WORKBOOK

The Development Of The
New Testament

By Arthur M. Ogden

Copyright © Arthur M. Ogden, 1995-2026 All rights reserved.
No part of this book may be reproduced in any form
without written consent from the publisher.

Printed in the United States of America.

Third Edition, 2026

ISBN 978-0-9646497-7-4

Questions and scripture quotations are based on the
English Standard Version of the Bible, unless otherwise noted.

Content Editing By Amy Ogden Hatman

Cover Design & Layout By Stephen Lee Ogden

OGDEN
PUBLICATIONS

AOgden.com • ogdenpub@aogden.com

Introduction

The material contained in this workbook originally appeared as twelve articles in **Guardian of Truth Magazine** in 1982. The response was positive, and **Guardian of Truth Foundation** printed the material in booklet form in 1983. Though the booklet was not highly advertised, it was well received.

While the material is divided into thirteen chapters, it is not expected that the material can be covered in thirteen sessions. We recommend at least two sessions for each chapter and more if needed. This study can greatly enhance your learning experience.

Of this material, Earl E. Robertson wrote, June 9, 1983, *"This volume briefly gives the development of the Testament in a form and style conducive to a quick comprehension as to how the New Testament came into being. The dates, composition, purposes and other valuable information of all the books of the New Testament are covered in this volume. We feel this booklet will be used often in many households among Christians in a very beneficial manner."*

Ogden Publications is happy to make this material available to you in this way. We believe you will find it a valuable asset in your study of God's Word. To this end we dedicate this work.

Arthur M. Ogden - 1995

This third edition is a revision of the previous versions of this work. A great many typos have been corrected and all scripture quotations have been changed to the *English Standard Version*. Some very minor editing has been done or a word or two was added to clarify a few places.

Alex D. Ogden - 2026

Table of Contents

LESSON TITLE	PAGE
01 **The Divine Technique**	01
02 **History's Role**	09
03 **The Historical Reconstruction**	16
04 **The Historical Reconstruction Cont.**	23
05 **The Primary & Literary Revelation**	30
06 **The Literary Revelation Continues**	37
07 **Paul's Literary Interlude**	44
08 **Paul's Prison Epistles**	51
09 **The Post Prison Epistles**	58
10 **The Post Prison Epistles Cont.**	65
11 **The Works of John**	72
12 **The Book of Revelation**	78
13 **The Testimony of History**	85
Notes	92

The History of the New Testament

Years	26	30	40	50	60	70
	JESUS' PERSONAL MINISTRY (JOHN 3.5 YEARS)	PENTECOST	PAUL SAVED / GENTILES / PAUL TO JERUSALEM	JAMES SLAIN / PAUL'S 1ST MISSIONARY JOURNEY	JERUSALEM CONFERENCE / PAUL'S 2ND MISSIONARY JOURNEY / PAUL'S 3RD MISSIONARY JOURNEY	PAUL IN PROSE / PAUL IN PRISON / FREED / DEATH
Roman Emperors		TIBERIUS CASAR 14-37 AD	CAIUS CASAR 37-41 AD	CLAUDIUS CASAR 41-54 AD	NERO CASAR 54-68 AD	VESPASIAN / ROMAN-JEWISH WAR 66-70 AD
Governors of Judea		PILATE 14-37 AD	MARCELLUS 37-41 AD / KING AGRIPPA I 41-44 AD / FADUS	CUMANUS 48-52 AD / ALEXANDER	FELIX 52-60 AD / FESTUS 60 / ALBINUS 62 / FLORUS 64	
The Revelation of the New Testament	JERUSALEM ON PENTECOST *Miracles*	THE ERA OF THE HOLY SPIRIT / DIRECT REVELATION / WORD OF MOUTH ONLY / "ALL TRUTH" REVEALED			INSPIRED ORAL TEACHING / GIFTS *"In Part"* *Spiritual Gifts*	BOOK *"Perfect"* THE WRITTEN WORD

iii

The Chronology of the New Testament

DATE	DESCRIPTION	NEW TESTAMENT
26 AD	Pilate Begins Rule of Judea	
	The Ministry of John The Baptist	
27		Jesus Taught
		The People
28		& Prepared
		His Apostles
29		
		Holy Spirit
30	Crucifixion - Resurrection - Ascension **PENTECOST**	Came (Baptism)
31	Stephen Is Stoned & The Saints Scatter	
32	Philip Preached in Samaria - Ethiopian Converted	Laying on of Hands Holy Spirit Imparted
33	Saul's Conversion - Saul in Arabia	
34		**God's**
35		**Word**
		In
36	Saul's 1st Missionary Journey to Jerusalem	**Inspired**
	Saul Returned to Tarsus	**Men**
37	Peter Raised Dorcus from the Dead	
38	Household of Cornelius Converted	
39		2nd Case of Holy Spirit Baptism
40		
41	Barnabas Sent to Antioch	
42	Paul Joins Barnabas in Antioch	
43		**God's**
44	Paul & Barnabas Delivered Contribution to Judea	**Word**
	Herod Agrippa Slew James	**In**
45	**Paul's 1st Missionary Journey**	**Inspired**
	Cyprus	**Men**
46	Antioch (Pisidia)	**Only**
	Iconium	
47	Lystra	
	Derbe	
48	Paul & Barnabas Return to Antioch (Syria)	
	Conflict With Judaizing Teachers	
49		

Continued →

The Chronology of the New Testament

DATE	DESCRIPTION	NEW TESTAMENT
49 AD	Jerusalem Conference	Written Word (Conference Epistle)
50	**Paul's 2nd Missionary Journey** Epistle Delivered / Churches of Galatia Confirmed	
51	Paul in Europe: Philippi, Thessalonica, Berea, Athens & Corinth	
52		1st Thessalonians
53	Paul Travels to Ephesus, Jerusalem & Antioch **Paul's 3rd Missionary Journey** Revists Churches of Galatia Begins Work in Ephesus	2nd Thessalonians
54		
55		Galatians
56		
57	Paul Visits Troas, Macedonia & Achaia Winters in Corinth	1st Corinthians 2nd Corinthians
58	Paul Travels to Jerusalem with Contribution Paul is Mobbed in Jerusalem Paul is Imprisoned in Casarea	Romans Matthew?
59		Matthew?
60	Paul Appealed to Casar Before Festus Paul's Travel to Rome as a Prisoner	Mark? James?
61	**PAUL'S FIRST ROMAN IMPRISONMENT**	Gospel of John? Luke
62	Paul Released from Roman Imprisonment	Philippians - Ephesians Colossians - Philemon
63	**Paul's Final Missionary Journey** Crete - Jerusalem?	Acts - Hebrews
64	Asia (Leaves Timothy at Ephesus) Macedonia Achaia Troas	1 Peter Titus - 1 Timothy 1,2,3 John 2 Peter
65	**Paul's 2nd Roman Imprisonment**	Jude 2 Timothy Revelation
66	——— THE ROMAN - JEWISH WAR ———	
67	Vespasian's Galilean Campaign	**God's Word In The Inspired Book**
68		
69	Titus Sent to Complete the War	
70	——— THE DESTRUCTION OF JERUSALEM ———	

LESSON 01

THE DIVINE TECHNIQUE

The Bible is the world's most marvelous book. It, and its subject matter, is the wonder of the ages. The minds of men have feasted upon its contents more than upon any other work. Through the years it has constantly been the world's best seller, remaining not only the oldest but the only production of antiquity to be in popular use and demand. More copies of the Bible have been sold than any other production known to man. The storms of time, criticism, infidelity, hatred and indifference have beat upon it, yet it lives on unscathed by the forces that would have destroyed any other work. Surely this Book of books is what it claims to be, the Word of God, and has been preserved for us through the centuries by divine providence.

Where did the Bible come from? How did it get here? Is it the fullness of God's revelation for us today? Can it be trusted, and can we read and study it with confidence? These questions and many more are of utmost importance. If the Bible is from God, every living soul must know it, for our eternal destiny depends upon it. In reality, there are no excuses for ignorance in the matter, for countless are the volumes written in response to these questions. It is doubtful that any one person in a lifetime could read and comprehend all of the contributions made in support of the Divine source of this Holy Book.

In this study, we shall look at the New Testament portion of the Bible, its revelation, development, production, reproduction, authority and completeness. Our study is based on the internal evidence of the New Testament books themselves. Such a study will be useful in many ways. (1) It will establish the fact that God miraculously guided men in the production of the New Testament Scriptures. (2) It will help us to fix the precise point in history when the revelation of divine truth was completed both *orally* and in *writing*. (3) It will substantiate the authority of the New Testament Scriptures. (4) It will solidify the twenty-seven books of the New Testament as the completeness of God's Word revealed in these last days (Heb.1:1,2). (5) It will fix each book in its relationship to its history and purpose, and enhance our understanding of each of them. (6) It will lead to a greater appreciation for the New Testament Scriptures and for our early brethren who produced, reproduced and preserved them for us. (7) It will produce greater faith in the New Testament Scriptures as the Word of God.[1]

The Old Testament Scriptures

To study the revelation, development and reproduction of the Old Testament Scriptures would be an interesting work, though we must refrain from that laborious task in this study. We would call attention, however, to the fact that the thirty-nine books which constitute our Old Testament Scriptures were in existence, production and common use while Jesus walked upon earth. They were read in the synagogues every Sabbath (Acts 15:21), and Jesus made it His practice on Sabbath days to enter the synagogues in order to read publicly from them and teach the people (Lk.4:14-20). Often, He quoted from them calling them *"the scriptures"* (Matt.21:42; Jn.5:39). Most of the Old Testament books are either quoted from or referred to in some way in the New Testament.[2] *"men spoke from God as they were carried along by the Holy Spirit"* (2 Pet.1:21). In addition, the Old Testament Scriptures had been translated from Hebrew into Greek in what is known as the Septuagint Version. This work began during the reign of Ptolemy II of Egypt (285–247 B.C.) and was finished sometime within the next one hundred years.[3] All of the Old Testament Scriptures, as we know them, were in existence and in popular use during Jesus' personal ministry.

A New Covenant Promised

Many hundreds of years before Jesus was born, God promised through the prophets that He would make a New Covenant. *"Behold, the days are coming, declares the LORD, when I will make a new covenant with the house of Israel and the house of Judah"* (Jer.31:31). *"And I will make with you an everlasting covenant, my steadfast, sure love for David"* (Isa.55:3; cf.61:8; Jer.32:40). *"I will make with them a covenant of peace"* (Ezek.34:25; cf.37:20-26). The Lord said to Moses, *"I will raise up for them a prophet like you from among their brothers. And I will put my words in his mouth, and he shall speak to them all that I command him"* (Deut.18:18,19). In anticipation and expectation, God's faithful people in Israel awaited the arrival of the Prophet like Moses who would mediate the New Covenant (cf.Jn.1:21,23; 6:14; 7:40).

Jesus The Prophet Of Whom Moses & The Prophets Wrote

As Jesus was beginning His personal ministry, He called Philip to follow Him. Philip was so impressed that he found Nathanael and said, *"We have found him of whom Moses in the Law and also the prophets* wrote, *Jesus of Nazareth, the son of Joseph"* (Jn.1:45). God had said, *"I will put my words in his mouth, and he shall speak to them all that I command him"* (Deut.18:18). Jesus fulfilled the demands of this prophecy. Of Himself he said, *"the Son can do nothing of his own accord, but only what he sees the Father doing. For whatever the Father does, that the Son does likewise"* (Jn.5:19). *"My teaching is not mine, but his who sent me"* (Jn.7:16). *"The words that I say to you I do not speak on my own authority, but the Father who dwells in me does his works"* (Jn.14:10). *"I have given (the apostles, AMO) them the words that you gave me...I have given them your word"* (Jn.17:8,14). *"The one who rejects me and does not receive my words has a judge; the word that I have spoken will judge him on the last day. For I have not spoken on my own authority, but the Father who sent me has himself given me a commandment—what to say and what to speak... What I say, therefore, I say as the Father has told me"* (Jn.12:48-50). So, Jesus was that Prophet God promised through whom He would reveal His New Covenant. Philip reached the proper conclusion.

The Revelation Technique

Jesus received of the Father what He should speak, and gave those words unto His apostles with assurance He would speak through them (Jn.12:48-50; 17:8). He said, *"whoever receives the one I send receives me, and whoever receives me receives the one who sent me"* (Jn.13:20). Again, *"The one who hears you hears me, and the one who rejects you rejects me, and the one who rejects me rejects him who sent me"* (Lk.10:16). With these assurances, Jesus established the technique for the revelation of the New Testament. He would put the words received from the Father into the hands of His chosen apostles, His messengers to the people (cf.2 Cor.5:18-20; 4:6,7).

The Promise Of The Holy Spirit

During His personal ministry, Jesus taught His disciples giving them the words the Father gave Him, though it is clear He did not teach them all things. On the evening of His betrayal and approximately twelve hours before His crucifixion, He said to His disciples (Judas excluded), *"I still have many things to say to you, but you cannot bear them now. When the Spirit of truth comes, he will guide you into all the truth"* (Jn.16:12,13). Earlier that evening, Jesus informed His disciples that He was going to His Father (Jn.13:33,36; 14:4,12,28; 16:10), but promised He would not leave them comfortless, or as orphans. *"And I will ask the Father, and he will give you another Helper, to be with you forever, even the Spirit of truth... I will not leave you as orphans; I will come to you"*

(Jn.14:16-18). Again, He said, *"But the Helper, the Holy Spirit, whom the Father will send in my name, he will teach you all things and bring to your remembrance all that I have said to you"* (Jn.14:26). Again, *"But when the Helper comes, whom I will send to you from the Father, the Spirit of truth, who proceeds from the Father, he will bear witness about me. And you also will bear witness, because you have been with me from the beginning"* (Jn.15:26,27). So, the continuation of the revelation of the New Testament through God's Prophet was to be expedited by the Holy Spirit sent from the Father by Jesus Christ. The Holy Spirit (1) would bring all things to the remembrance of the apostles, which Jesus had taught them, (2) teach them all things and, therefore, (3) guide them into all truth. The Spirit served only as the agent through whom the Covenant was revealed; *"he will not speak on his own authority, but whatever he hears he will speak, and he will declare to you the things that are to come. He will glorify me, for he will take what is mine and declare it to you"* (Jn.16:13,14). With these provisions made for the continuation of the revelation of the New Testament, Jesus died the next day. Three days later, He was raised from the dead. After forty days, in which He demonstrated His resurrection by many infallible proofs (Acts 1:1-3), Jesus ascended to heaven promising to send the Holy Spirit (Acts 1:8,9).

The Holy Spirit At Work

Ten days after Jesus ascended to heaven, on the day called Pentecost, the Holy Spirit fell upon the apostles in the city of Jerusalem to begin His work (Acts 2:1-4,33). He came first to fulfill the first half of God's promise to *"pour out my Spirit on all flesh"* (Joel 2:28; cf.Acts 2:17). The Holy Spirit fell upon the Jews on Pentecost. The second half of the promise was fulfilled seven or eight years later in Caesarea when the Holy Spirit fell upon the Gentiles at the house of Cornelius (Acts 10:44,45). The Holy Spirit falling upon the household of Cornelius corresponds to the baptism of the Holy Spirit on the day of Pentecost (cf.Matt.3:11; Acts 1:4,5; 11:15,16). Secondly, the Holy Spirit came on Pentecost endowing the apostles with the full power of their office, guiding them into all truth and clothing them with powers to confirm the word (Jn.16:13; Lk.24:49; Acts 1:5,6,8; Mk.16:19,20; Heb.2:3,4). Under the power of the Holy Spirit, the apostles, with Peter as the chief spokesman, preached the gospel on Pentecost and in the days following (Acts 4:8,31). They preached first in Jerusalem (Acts 6:8-10) and then in the various places to which they were directed (Acts 7:55; 9:5-7,29,39). *"They went out and preached everywhere, while the Lord worked with them and confirmed the message by accompanying signs"* (Mk.16:20).

Approximately three years after Pentecost, the Lord Jesus appeared unto Saul of Tarsus near Damascus (Acts 9:1-16) for the expressed purpose of preparing him to be an apostle (Acts 9:15,16; 22:14; 26:15-18). He said of himself that he was *"one untimely born"* and *"unworthy to be called an apostle, because"* he said, *"I persecuted the church of God"* (1 Cor.15:8,9). Nonetheless, he received the Holy Spirit (Acts 9:17; Gal.1:11-13,16,17) and was fully endowed as an apostle so that he was *"not in the least inferior to these super-apostles"* (2 Cor.11:5; 12:11). The message he proclaimed corresponded perfectly with that preached by the other apostles (cf.Gal.1:11,12,16-2:10; Acts 15:1-31). This demonstrated that, though he was not with the Lord on earth and did not communicate with the Twelve, the Word received by revelation did not differ from that received by the Twelve. He, too, was guided into all truth (Acts 20:27), and on whomsoever he laid his hands they received the Holy Spirit and the accompanying gifts (Acts 19:6; 2 Tim.1:6). This demonstrates the force and power of the Holy Spirit in fulfilling the mission of revealing the New Testament to man.

The New Testament *"was declared at first by the Lord, and it was attested to us by those who heard, while God also bore witness by signs and wonders and various miracles and by gifts of the Holy Spirit distributed according to his will"* (Heb.2:3,4). The revelation of the Word, the confirmation by the signs, wonders, miracles and the various gifts were all manifestations of the Holy Spirit at work. Nine different gifts were employed by the Holy Spirit in revealing the New Covenant to the early Christians (1 Cor.12:1-11). They were imparted by the laying on of the apostles' hands (Acts 8:14-19). Their design was to supply each Christian possessing them with a portion of the Word (cf.1 Cor.13:8,9). This enabled each congregation to have the fullness of God's truth available to them. In this way, in the days before the New Testament was written, the early Christians had God's complete Word accessible to them through inspired men (cf.1 Jn.2:20,21,27).

Lesson Exercises

Fill In The Blank

1. God said, "I ... will put my _____ in his mouth, and he shall speak to them _____ that I _____ him" (Deut.18:18).

2. "The _____ that I say to you I do not speak on my own authority, but the _____ who _____ in me does his _____" (Jn.14:10).

3. "The one who _____ me and _____ ____ _____ my words has a _____; the _____ that I have spoken will _____ him" (Jn.12:48).

4. "I still have many things to _____ to you... When the _____ of truth comes, he will guide you into _____ the _____" (Jn.16:12,13).

5. "But the _____, the _____ _____, ... he will _____ you _____ things" (Jn.14:26).

6. "... he will take what is _____ and declare it to _____" (Jn.16:15).

7. "And they went out and preached everywhere, while the Lord worked with them and _____ the _____ by accompanying _____" (Mk.16:20).

8. "For I did not shrink from _____ to you the whole _____ of God" (Acts 20:27).

9. The N.T. "... was _____ at first by the Lord, and it was _____ to us by those who heard" (Heb.2:3).

10. "while _____ also bore witness by _____ and _____, and _____ _____ and by _____ of the Holy Spirit" (Heb.2:4).

Lesson 01 - The Divine Technique

Questions

1. How many books in the Bible? _____ O. T.? _____

2. How many O. T. books are quoted from in the N.T.? _____

3. Explain how a Bible book came into existence:

4. What three divisions of the O.T. did Jesus recognize (cf.Lk.24:44)?

5. What element in scripture distinguishes them from other writings?

6. Where could one go every Saturday to hear the scriptures?

7. In what language were the O.T. Scriptures originally written?

8. What is the Septuagint Version?

9. The first translation of the O.T. was into what language?

10. Into what did Jesus say the Spirit would guide the apostles?

Match

1. Holy Spirit
2. Jesus
3. 250 B. C.
4. Spake in tongues
5. Deuteronomy 18:18-19
6. Acts 2:17-21
7. He that hears you
8. He that despises me
9. Preached on Pentecost
10. One born out of due season

_____ Septuagint
_____ John 12:48-50
_____ Hears me
_____ Peter
_____ The Prophet
_____ Despises God
_____ Paul
_____ Comforter
_____ Joel 2:28-32
_____ Apostles

True or False

1. _____ God promised Moses He would raise up another prophet from among his brethren like unto him.

2. _____ Philip told Nathanael he had found the prophet Moses wrote about.

3. _____ John the Baptist was the prophet like Moses.

4. _____ Jesus sent the apostles to guide the Holy Spirit into all truth.

5. _____ The Holy Spirit first came on the day of Pentecost.

6. _____ Peter said the Holy Spirit came on Pentecost to fulfill Isaiah 2:2-4.

7. _____ Peter was the chief spokesman on Pentecost.

8. _____ Signs followed the apostles confirming their word.

9. _____ Paul as an apostle was endowed with the Holy Spirit.

10. _____ The Holy Spirit will someday complete His work of guiding us into all truth.

Notes

LESSON 02

HISTORY'S ROLE

Did the Holy Spirit fully accomplish His work of guiding the apostles into *all truth*? If so, at what point in history was this work complete? To fully answer these questions, it is necessary to reconstruct, as best we can, the early history of Christianity up to and through the completion of the written New Testament. We can do this within reasonable limits by considering specific events related in the New Testament, which are also recorded and dated in secular history. We shall trace the inspired history of the early church as it relates to the history of the Roman Empire and the Roman rule of Judea. We will trace this history beginning with the personal ministry of John the Baptist (26 A.D.) up to the destruction of Jerusalem and the end of Israel as a nation (70 A.D.). We shall seek to pinpoint as many events as possible in the inspired account in relationship to this forty-four-year span. When we are finished, we will have clear insight into the process of the revelation of the New Testament as it developed.

The Roman Empire

The birth of Christ and the beginning of Christianity took place during the reign of the Roman kings as God promised many hundreds of years before (cf.Dan.2:31-44; 7:1-28). The determined efforts of Julius Caesar started the process that transformed the Roman Republic into an Empire, setting the stage for the fulfillment of the prophecies. He began the transformation as early as 61 B.C., and all but completed the task by 44 B.C. when he was murdered on the Senate floor.[4] Thirteen years later, Augustus, the nephew of Julius and his own hand-picked successor, ascended to the throne and completed the business of establishing the empire upon firm footing.[5] During the reign of Augustus (31 B.C.-14 A.D.), Jesus was born (Lk.2:1). Tiberius (14–37 A.D.) succeeded Augustus. During his reign, Jesus conducted His personal ministry, was crucified, ascended to heaven and began His church (Lk.3:1). Gaius (37–41 A.D.), better known by his nickname "Caligula," followed Tiberius. He is not mentioned in the Scriptures. Claudius (41–54 A.D.) came next. During his reign a great famine came upon the whole world (Acts 11:28). He also expelled all the Jews from Rome (Acts 18:2). Nero (54–68 A.D.) followed Claudius. Paul appealed to him for justice (Acts 25:11,12,21;

26:32; 27:24; 28:19; Phil.4:22). It was Nero who sent his most trusted General, Vespasian, to Judea in the spring of 67 A.D. to subdue the Jews. Nero died in June of 68 A.D., a victim of suicide. After several months of turmoil, Vespasian left the war in Judea to claim the throne for himself. He ascended to the throne in 69 A.D. and immediately sent Titus, his son, into Palestine to complete the work of subduing the Jews and destroying Jerusalem. He completed this work in 70 A.D.

The Judean Rulers

During the first one hundred years of the Roman Empire, Judea was ruled through administrators known as procurators (governors) and kings. Perhaps the most renown of all was Herod the Great. He was ruling (37–4 B.C.) when Jesus was born (Matt.2:1). Upon his death, his son Archelaus (4 B.C.–6 A.D.) ruled in his stead (Matt.2:22), but accusations against him before Caesar resulted in being banished from office.[6] He was followed by Procurators Coponius (6–9 A.D.), Marcus Ambibulus (9–12 A.D.), Annius Rufus (12–15 A.D.), Gratus (15–26 A.D.) and Pontius Pilate (26–36 A.D.).[7] The rule of Pilate covers the ministries of John the Baptist and Jesus (Lk.3:1), the crucifixion of Jesus (Matt.27:2) and the beginning and early history of the church. Marcellus (36–37 A.D.) and Marullus (37–41 A.D.) followed Pilate.[8] They are not mentioned in the sacred text. When Claudius came to the Roman throne, he sought to quell disorders erupting in Judea by making a Jew, Herod Agrippa I (41–44 A.D.) king over Judea.[9] This was the Herod who slew the apostle James and sought to kill Peter (Acts 12:1-4). He died after a three-year reign, smitten by God, because he accepted worship as a god (Acts 12:20-23).[10] After the death of Agrippa I, Fadus (44–46 A.D.), Alexander (46–48 A.D.) and Cumanus (48–52 A.D.) ruled Judea.[11] They are not mentioned in sacred history. Felix became the next procurator of Judea (52–60 A.D.).[12] His term of office was the longest of the governors after Pilate. It was before Felix that Paul appeared as a prisoner after being mobbed by the Jews in Jerusalem (Acts 23:24,26), and with whom he *"reasoned about righteousness and self-control and the coming judgment"* (Acts 24:25). Two years later Festus came to power (Acts 24:27). It was before Festus that Paul appealed to the protection of Caesar's supreme court (Acts 25:11), and by whom he was sent to Rome. The rule of Festus was short (60–62 A.D.), followed by Albinus (62–64 A.D.) and Florus (64–66 A.D.).[13] During the rule of Florus the Roman-Jewish War broke out. The last two governors are not mentioned in scripture.

The Inspired Account

We now have the historical background before us. Let us piece together the corresponding events of the sacred record in order to provide a structure upon which to build the historical account in relationship to time as revealed in our Bibles. In other words, let us set dates, within reasonable margins, upon the events as they transpired. This goal is attainable.

In approaching our project, let us bear in mind that the events revealed in sacred history must correspond perfectly with the events of secular history, and all other events, of its own record. For example, the date placed upon the martyrdom of the apostle James (Acts 12:1) must conform to the reign of Herod Agrippa 1 (41–44 A.D.; Acts 12:1-23). Again, the imprisonment of Paul (Acts 21:27-26:32) must take into account the rule of two governors, Felix (52–60 A.D.) and Festus (60–62 A.D.), with due respect to the revealed time periods specified. The times, places and events must all correspond to the known realities of the times. We must account for all specific time periods within their designated limits, or our conclusions will be worthless.

Fastened Guidelines

The existence of certain events abundantly aids our study of the history of Christ, the beginning of Christianity and the early history of the church. These events are so fixed by their nature that they become guidelines in placing dates upon other specific events. There are four that contribute heavily in this area:

First, the ministries of John the Baptist and Jesus must conform to the governorship of Pilate (Lk.3:1). Pilate ruled for ten years (26–36 A.D.).[14] Since the combined ministries of John and Jesus cover four years, they could not have begun earlier than 26 A.D. nor later than 32 A.D.

Second, the death of Christ took place during the week of Passover which occurred on the fourteenth day of Nisan (Abib) of each year (Lev.23:4-8; Num.9:2-5; 28:16; Ex.12). On this day, the Passover Lamb was slain and the Passover Feast observed in the evening. By nearly all scholarly accounts, the fourteenth of Nisan fell on Thursday of the Passion week. This is significant because this did not happen each year. According to a reliable source,[15] the only year in which the fourteenth of Nisan fell on Thursday, between 26 and 34 A.D., was the year 30 A.D. Since 26 is too early and 34 too late, 30 A.D. must of necessity be the year in which our Lord was crucified. This, corresponding to our calendar, places the death of Christ on April 6 or 7, (depending upon whether the crucifixion was on Thursday or Friday). This places His resurrection on April 9, His Ascension on May 18, and Pentecost, the day of the beginning of the church and Christianity, on May 28, 30 A.D.[16]

Third, the apostle Paul counts seventeen years between his conversion and the Jerusalem Conference (Gal.1:18; 2:1). This conference was convened to settle the question of circumcision (Acts 15; Gal.2:1-10). It was held sometime after Paul's *first* missionary journey (Acts 13-14), and before his *second* (Acts 16-18). Two to three years are needed to account for the events that transpired between Pentecost (Acts 2) and the conversion of Paul (Saul, Acts 9). The events following the Jerusalem conference must fit into the framework of ten or eleven years ending in the summer of 60 A. D. with the close of Felix' governorship (Acts 24:27). Therefore, the Jerusalem Conference could not have happened earlier than 49 A.D. or later than 50 A.D. This helps determine that the conversion of Paul occurred no earlier than 32, and no later than 34 A.D. (allowing for the possibility that a few months counted as one year).

Fourth, the transition of the Judean rule from Felix to Festus serves as the pivotal point for the history surrounding Paul from the time of his capture in Jerusalem (Acts 21:33) until his death. This transition took place in the summer of 60 A.D. Paul's arrest took place during the festivities surrounding the Feast of Pentecost (Acts 20:16). Twelve days after entering Jerusalem for the observance of Pentecost, Paul made his defense before Felix at Caesarea (Acts 24:11; cf.21:27; 24:1). Since Pentecost usually fell the last of May, Paul's imprisonment at Caesarea began in early June. He remained a prisoner at Caesarea for two years (Acts 24:27) before appearing before Festus and appealing to Caesar (Acts 25:11). Festus replaced Felix in the government at this time.

The exact time of this transition in government is essential to our project because it affects both the previous and subsequent histories. Indecision has existed through the years over whether Felix' rule ended in 60 or 61 A.D., perhaps because of different historical accounts. Felix, however, ruled for a number of years (Acts 24:10). Josephus places Felix' appointment with that of Agrippa II. Claudius appointed both to office in his twelfth year.[17] The appointment of Felix came in 52 A.D. Other historians record that Felix continued six years as procurator of Judea under Nero,[18] thus extending his rule to 60 A. D. Accepting this date simplifies the task of reconstruction.

Lesson Exercises

Fill In The Blank

1. Mary and Joseph were in Bethlehem when Jesus was born because _____ decreed that the world be taxed (Lk.2:1).

2. This was done when _____ was governor of _____ (Lk.2:2).

3. _____ the _____ ruled Judea at the time of Jesus' birth (Matt.2:1).

4. _____ governed Judea at the time of Jesus death (Matt.27:2).

5. _____ was the Jewish High Priest when Jesus was crucified (Jn.18:13).

6. Herod Agrippa I had the apostle _____ put to death (Acts 12:2).

7. When Paul was in Corinth, _____ was the deputy, or proconsul, of Achaia (Acts 18:12).

8. Paul preached the gospel to _____ who was also a Herod (Acts 26).

9. _____ and _____ were also governors of Judea (Acts 24:27).

10. Caesar, to whom Paul appealed in Acts 25:11, was _____.

Match

1. First Emperor of Rome
2. Second Emperor of Rome
3. Third Emperor of Rome
4. Fourth Emperor of Rome
5. Fifth Emperor of Rome
6. Sixth Emperor of Rome
7. Nero's most trusted General
8. Vespasian's son
9. Date of Julius Caesar's death
10. Date of Jerusalem's destruction

___ Vespasian
___ 70 A.D.
___ Nero
___ Augustus
___ Titus
___ 44 B.C.
___ Julius Caesar
___ Claudius
___ Tiberius
___ Caius

Questions

1. The ministries of John the Baptist & Jesus happened during the rule of what governor?

2. Jesus' ministry covered approximately how many years?

3. How long had the temple been in building in John 2:20?

4. In what year did Herod begin this work on the temple?*

5. When did Jesus say He would be crucified (Matt.26:2)?

6. On what day did Passover come each year (cf.Ex.12; Lev.23:4-8; Num.9:2-5; 28:16)?

7. In what year, according to our calendar, was Jesus crucified?

8. When was Jesus resurrected from the grave?

9. How many days following Jesus' resurrection before His ascension (Acts 1:3)?

10. On what day did the New Testament order begin?

---

* To answer this question, you will need to do some research in other sources. Check Bible Dictionaries, Josephus, and I.S.B.E. under *Temple* or *Herod's Temple*.

Lesson 02 - History's Role

True or False

1. _____ History is of no benefit in understanding the Bible.

2. _____ Augustus was Emperor when Jesus was born.

3. _____ Nero was Emperor during the ministry of Jesus.

4. _____ The church had its beginning in 33 A.D.?

5. _____ There were 17 years between Paul's conversion and the Jerusalem Conference (Gal.1:18-2:1).

6. _____ The Bible records 3 missionary journeys of Paul.

7. _____ Dionysius Exiguus developed what is known as "carbon dating."

8. _____ Paul was a prisoner at Cesarea for two years.

9. _____ In order to escape the wrath of Caesar, Paul appealed unto the Jews.

10. _____ Paul was a prisoner in Rome for two years.

Notes

LESSON 03

THE HISTORICAL RECONSTRUCTION

We have established a structure upon which to build our thesis. Let us now proceed to fit the pieces to that structure so we can provide the foundation upon which to observe the revelation of the New Testament in relation to this history. Our counting of time begins at Pentecost, May 28, 30 A.D., and will continue as far as the inspired record will allow.

30-33 A.D.

Specific time periods cannot be determined during the first three years after Pentecost (Acts 2-8). We know the disciples enjoyed a period of uninterrupted teaching and favor among the people following Pentecost (Acts 2:42-43,46-47). This period of tolerance may have lasted from a few days to a few weeks, or months. Then, Peter and John healed *"the lame man"* (Acts 3) which became the pretext for the first conflict with the authorities (Acts 4). By this time the church had grown from 3,000 persons to 5,000 men (Acts 4:4). This could indicate the passing of several months. The company of disciples was now large enough to command attention from the authorities. Peter and John were arrested, threatened and released with hope that the flames of enthusiasm among the disciples would die and the movement fail (Acts 4:3,21). Instead, the disciples prayed for strength and united under the banner of the cross and the power of the Holy Spirit. They even sold their possessions, contributed to a common fund from which the whole number was sustained, and continued faithfully in the face of the threatening powers (Acts 4:5-11). Their numbers continued to grow (Acts 5:12-16) until the Jewish authorities had to act. The apostles were arrested (Acts 5:18), but the council was restrained from murderous action against them by Gamaliel. They were again threatened, beaten, commanded to refrain from teaching in the name of Jesus, and released (Acts 5:33-40). The disciples, however, were not deterred by these threats. They continued to teach and preach daily in the temple (Acts 5:42). During these days, seven men were chosen to serve in the ministration of the tables (Acts 6:1-8). One of them, Stephen, was martyred which began the attempt of the Jewish authorities to stamp out Christianity (Acts 6:9-7:60). We do not know how much time passed in the development of these events. It is likely that as much as six to nine months passed from Pentecost to the death of Stephen, and perhaps even longer.

After the death of Stephen, attempts to discourage Christianity and bring it to an end accelerated (Acts 8:1-3; 26:9-11). Saul became one of the chief instigators of this persecution. Within a short time, the disciples were scattered from Jerusalem into *"regions of Judea and Samaria"* (Acts 8:1). Philip, who was one of the seven, went to Samaria and preached the gospel to them (Acts 8:5-13). Peter and John later joined him there, also preaching in the villages of the Samaritans (Acts 8:25). Philip, under the direction of the angel of the Lord, moved to the south to convert the Ethiopian Eunuch who had been to Jerusalem to worship (Acts 8:26-39). The feast attended by the Eunuch is not clear. The pattern of Jewish worship and the development of the divine purpose (Acts 1:8) would indicate that his conversion occurred following one of the spring festivals (Passover or Pentecost) in 31 or 32 A.D.

Following the events of Acts 8, the gospel spread throughout all the regions of Judea and Samaria, Phoenicia, Cyprus, Antioch, Damascus and other cities of the world (Acts 8:40; 9:10; 11:19; 26:11). During the months following the scattering of the saints, Saul followed them into these foreign cities (Acts 26:11). His journey to Damascus apparently was not his first intrusion into a foreign city to persecute the church. We need time to account for the establishment, growth and spread of Christianity into these foreign cities. However, we cannot register Saul's trip to Damascus (Acts 9) later than 34 A.D. without upsetting his own inspired timetable (cf.Gal.1:18; 2:1). Therefore, we believe the conversion of Saul took place sometime during 33 or early 34 A.D.

33-44 A.D.

After the conversion of Saul, the historical record begins to build around him. Immediately following his conversion, Saul went into Arabia (Gal.1:17). Then, after three years, he went up to Jerusalem (Gal.1:18) and, after a brief stay there, went to Tarsus (Acts 9:30; Gal.1:18-21). These events happened no later than 37 A.D. In the months following, *"the church throughout all Judea and Galilee and Samaria had peace and was being built up"* (Acts 9:31). Sometime following, Peter raised Dorcus from the dead (Acts 9:36-43) and preached the gospel to the Gentiles at the house of Cornelius (Acts 10). We do not know at what point in history the Gentiles first received the word, but it had to be after 36 A.D. and before the winter of 39-40 A.D. At that time the Jews throughout Palestine were enraged against all Romans. Gaius, the emperor, sent Petronius to Judea to erect his image in the temple at Jerusalem.[19] This angered the Jews. It is doubtful that a Roman centurion, particularly one of the Italian Band, could receive a commendation from the Jews (cf.Acts 10:22) after 39 A.D. without developing serious difficulties within his own ranks. For this reason, we feel the conversion of Cornelius occurred no earlier than 37 A.D. nor later than the fall of 39 A.D.

Following the conversion of the Gentiles in Caesarea, a period of growth and expansion ensued in which Gentiles in many places, particularly in Antioch, were converted to Christ (Acts 11:19-22). Upon hearing the good news of the growth in these regions, the brethren in Jerusalem sent Barnabas that he should go as far as Antioch (Acts 11:22). Antioch was three hundred miles from Jerusalem and, if Barnabas spent any time in other places as is indicated, he could have spent several months in travels prior to coming to Antioch. We suggest that he was sent in late 41 or early 42 A.D. After spending some time in Antioch, Barnabas went to Tarsus, found Paul and brought him back to Antioch to assist in the work there (Acts 11:23-26). Returning to Antioch in 43 A.D., they assembled with the church *"a whole year"* (Acts 11:26) before going to Judea and Jerusalem with a contribution for the brethren in Judea (Acts 11:27-30). While they were in Jerusalem, Herod Agrippa I killed the apostle James and sought to kill Peter (Acts 12:1-19). These events happened in 44 A.D., before and after the Passover and the Feast of Unleavened Bread, which usually fell around the first of April each year. Afterward, Agrippa returned to Caesarea where he died, struck down by God (Acts 12:20-23). He had reigned three years, having been appointed to his office by Emperor Claudius shortly after coming to power early in 41 A.D.[20] After these things, Paul and Barnabas returned to Antioch (Acts 11:24,25).

44–50 A.D.

After Paul and Barnabas returned to Antioch, the Holy Spirit called them for the first missionary journey (Acts 13:1-3). The context indicates nothing regarding this date, so we suggest that the call came early in 45 A.D. and took them on a journey that possibly lasted three or more years. The first phase of this work took them to the Island of Cyprus, the homeland of Barnabas (Acts 13:4-13; cf.4:36). They covered the whole island, establishing churches (Acts 15:36,39)—a task that could have taken from a few months to a whole year. After leaving Cyprus, they sailed to Perga in Pamphylia, located in the southern regions of Asia Minor (Acts 13:13). From Perga they traveled to Antioch in Pisidia where a large number of Gentiles believed (Acts 13:48), *"And the word of the Lord was spreading throughout the whole region"* (Acts 13:49). Their stay at Antioch could have been a few weeks or even a few months. From there they went to Iconium where both Jews and Greeks believed and there they abode a *"long time"* (Acts 14:1-3). Apparently, they stayed here several months, perhaps a year or longer. From Iconium they traveled to Lystra (Acts 14:8). Again, there are no indications of how long they remained in Lystra though converts were made there (Acts 14:20). This was the home of Timothy, whose mother and grandmother, no doubt, were converted at this time (Acts 16:1,2; 2 Tim.1:5). From Lystra they went to Derbe where they preached the gospel and taught many (Acts 14:21). From this point Paul and Barnabas revisited the established churches, confirmed them and ordained elders in every church (Acts 14:22,23). Paul and Barnabas returned to Antioch in Syria when they had completed their work. The time consumed by this journey is unknown. The territory covered, the number of conversions, the strengthening of the disciples and the ordaining of elders in the churches indicates at least three years were needed to accomplish this work. We suggest that this journey began in 45 and was completed sometime in 48 A.D.

Following the *first* missionary journey, Paul and Barnabas returned to Antioch where *"they remained no little time with the disciples"* (Acts 14:28). During this interim, Judaizing teachers from Jerusalem came into the regions around Syria and Antioch teaching that *"Unless you are circumcised according to the custom of Moses, you cannot be saved"* (Acts 15:1). They were seeking to bind the Jewish law and practices upon the Gentile converts. The matter stirred much discussion and debate. Paul and Barnabas opposed them (Acts 15:2; Gal.2:4,5). The matter grew so severe that Paul and Barnabas, with the support of the church at Antioch, went to Jerusalem to settle the matter with the apostles and elders of the church there (Acts 15:2,3). The matter was settled and an epistle written to Gentile converts in Antioch, Syria and Cilicia (Acts 15:22-29). **This epistle was the first part of the New Testament written by inspiration!** Following this conference, Paul and Barnabas, accompanied by Judas and Silas, returned to Antioch with the epistle and confirmation of its contents. After *"some time"* (Acts 15:33), a visit to Antioch by Peter and others (Gal.2:11-14) *"and after some days"* (Acts 15:36), Paul began his *second* missionary journey (Acts 15:40,41).

The time elements involved—the return of Barnabas and Paul to Antioch from Jerusalem in the summer of 44 A.D., the time spent in Antioch before their call for the *first* missionary journey, the approximate three years required for the journey and the time spent in Antioch after returning from the journey—suggest that the Jerusalem Conference occurred near the end of the fifth decade A.D. Adding the previously stated factors—namely, (1) the seventeen years designated by Paul as transpiring between his conversion and the conference (Gal.1:18; 2:1) and (2) the ten years needed to conduct Paul's *second* missionary journey (3 years), *third* missionary journey (5 years) and imprisonment to the end of Felix' governorship in 60 A.D. (2 years, Acts 24:27)—confirms that the Jerusalem Conference was not conducted later than early 50 A.D., with the most probable date late 49 A.D. We suggest 49 A.D. because there appears to be more time available for the conference at that time.

Historical Reconstruction continues in Lesson 4.

Lesson Exercises

Multiple Choice

1. Following his conversion, Paul went into **(Damascus, Arabia, Egypt)**.

2. When Paul was threatened by the Jews in Jerusalem he was sent to **(Tarsus, Antioch, Arabia)**.

3. Paul later joined **(Judas, Barnabas, Silas)** at Antioch.

4. Paul went on his first missionary journey to **(Europe, Galatia, Asia)**.

5. Following this missionary journey, Paul returned to **(Jerusalem, Antioch, Jericho)**.

6. Judaizing teachers came to Antioch from **(Damascus, Tarsus, Jerusalem)**.

7. The Judaizing teachers were seeking to bind **(baptism, foot-washing, circumcision)**.

8. The **(Sanhedrin, church, priests)** in Jerusalem met to settle the question.

9. The apostles and elders were joined by the **(High Priest, Bishop, Holy Spirit)** in writing a letter to the churches.

10. **(Luke & Silas, Judas & Silas, Timothy & Silas)** accompanied Paul & Barnabas in delivering the epistle.

Lesson 03 - The Historical Reconstruction

Questions

1. Explain the method the Lord used to facilitate universal evangelization.

2. What institutional leftover from the law aided the early Christians in this work?

3. Where were the apostles in the early days of Christianity?

4. Who was the first evangelist to go on a preaching trip?

5. What apostles followed him?

6. Which apostle opened the way for the preaching of the gospel to the Gentiles?

7. To what city did Philip go and make his home there?

8. What church in Syria became the center for much activity?

9. Who was sent out from Jerusalem to go as far as Antioch?

10. Who joined Barnabas in the work at Antioch?

Match

1. Eunuch
2. Conversion of Saul
3. Conversion of Cornelius
4. Paul's 1st Missionary Journey
5. The Jerusalem Conference
6. Petronius
7. Gaius
8. Philip
9. Home of Timothy
10. Antioch

_____ About 45 A.D.
_____ Caesar's image
_____ Samaria
_____ Syria
_____ 33–34 A.D.
_____ Lystra
_____ About 49 A.D.
_____ Ethiopia
_____ Roman Emperor
_____ 37–39 A.D.

True or False

1. _____ The church enjoyed a brief period of favor from the Jews following Pentecost.

2. _____ Difficulties came after Peter and James healed the lame man.

3. _____ The persecutions slowed the progress of the saints.

4. _____ The first recorded Christian martyr was Stephen.

5. _____ Saul of Tarsus was ringleader in the persecutions.

6. _____ Stephen was first to preach the gospel in Samaria.

7. _____ Following the conversion of the Samaritans, the gospel spread throughout Judea, Samaria, Phoenicia, Cyprus, Antioch, Damascus and beyond.

8. _____ Saul went into these cities persecuting the saints.

9. _____ After the conversion of Saul, the historical record builds around Peter.

10. _____ Paul (Saul) and Barnabas teamed up to carry the gospel into foreign fields.

Notes

LESSON 04

THE HISTORICAL RECONSTRUCTION CONTINUED

Our reconstruction of the biblical account began on Pentecost in 30 A.D. The previous lesson carried us through the Jerusalem Conference, a period of approximately 20 years. In this lesson, we continue the biblical reconstruction through the life of Paul.

50–53 A.D.

The *second* missionary journey of Paul began at Antioch sometime following the Jerusalem Conference. This journey took Paul and Silas (Acts 15:40) *"through Syria and Cilicia, strengthening the churches"* (Acts 15:41) and delivering the decrees of the apostles and elders at Jerusalem regarding the Judaizing teachers (Acts 15:23-29; 16:4). Passing *"through the region of Phrygia and Galatia"* (Acts 16:6) and being forbidden by the Holy Spirit to preach the word in Asia, Mysia and Bithynia (Acts 16:6,7), they came to Troas (Acts 16:8). Here Luke joined their company (Acts 16:10). The time consumed from Antioch to Troas cannot be determined. It could have required a year or more. From Troas Paul's company crossed the Aegean Sea to Europe. They preached the gospel first in Philippi. They then went to Thessalonica and Berea before going to Athens and Corinth. The time spent in Europe on this journey is somewhat easier to follow than other periods, though the exact time at several places cannot be ascertained.

With the exception of Corinth, where Paul spent a year and six months (Acts 18:11), it appears that he spent the longest period in Philippi. There are several reasons for this conclusion: (1) The expression *"many days"* (Acts 16:18), used in connection with his stay in Philippi, usually denotes an extended period of time.[21] (2) Paul does not show the concern over the development of the Philippians that he showed over the Thessalonians, to whom he wrote two epistles shortly after leaving them. This indicates that Philippi's progress surpassed that of Thessalonica. (3) Paul's commendation of their early strength, growth and development (cf.Phil.1:5,6; 4:1-3,9,10,15-17) indicates that sufficient time was spent with them to ground them in the faith during his stay. (4) Paul left no one at Philippi to strengthen them as he did the Bereans, where he left

Silas and Timothy (Acts 17:14), or the Thessalonians, to whom he sent Timothy shortly after leaving them (1 Thess.3:1,2). The only one of Paul's company who stayed in Philippi was Luke, the author of the book of Acts. Luke joined them at Troas. His presence with Paul at Philippi can be traced by his use of the first-person plural pronouns *we* and *us* (cf.Acts 16:11,12,13,15,16,17). Luke's presence with Paul and his company is not mentioned again until the spring of 58 A.D., when Paul left Philippi for Jerusalem (Acts 20:5,6). His being in Philippi then, does not appear to be as an evangelist. The length of Paul's stay in Philippi was probably near three months.

From Philippi, Paul's company traveled to Thessalonica where they spent approximately one month (Acts 17:14). About the same amount of time was spent at Berea (Acts 17:10-14). From there Paul journeyed to Athens where Timothy and Silas joined him shortly (Acts 17:15,16; cf.1 Thess.3:1-3). This would have consumed no less than another month. Paul then moved on to Corinth where he spent a full year and six months (Acts 18:11). When his work in Corinth ended, he went to Ephesus accompanied by Acquila and Priscilla (Acts 18:18). Here he taught briefly but due to his desire to *"keep the feast that cometh in Jerusalem"* (Acts 18:21 KJV), probably the feast of Passover, he left Ephesus for Jerusalem. From Jerusalem he returned to Antioch from where he began this *second* journey (Acts 18:22). All in all, no less than three years were required for the *second* journey; therefore, his visit to Antioch at the close of this journey came in the summer of 53 A.D.

53-58 A.D.

"After spending some time there," Paul left Antioch beginning his *third* missionary journey. He *"went from one place to the next through the region of Galatia and Phrygia, strengthening all the disciples"* (Acts 18:23). Then, returning to Ephesus, he continued the work previously begun. This phase of the journey probably took him from six to nine months, placing him in Ephesus around May of 54 A.D. Later, Paul reflects upon having spent three years in Ephesus (Acts 20:31). Evidently, he counted three years from the time of his return to the city because he indicates an uninterrupted stay. He said, *"I did not cease night or day to admonish every one with tears."* Paul taught three months in the synagogue, and two years in the school of Tyrannus (Acts 19:8-10). In addition, Paul strongly implies an imprisonment (cf.2 Cor.6:5), a sentence of death (2 Cor.1:8-11) and a casting to the beasts (1 Cor.15:32). These, and other activities, take time. It is likely that Paul spent three full years in Ephesus after returning to the city on his *third* missionary journey.

Of the end of Paul's stay in Ephesus, Luke records, *"Now after these events Paul resolved in the Spirit to pass through Macedonia and Achaia and go to Jerusalem... And having sent into Macedonia two of his helpers, Timothy and Erastus, he himself stayed in Asia for a while"* (Acts 19:21,22). This stated purpose on the part of Paul is again reflected in his first epistle to Corinth, which is known to have been written from Ephesus (cf.1 Cor.16:8,19). In this letter, he proposed that after passing through Macedonia he would come to them and suggested the possibility of spending the winter (1 Cor.16:5,6). His plans were to leave Ephesus after Pentecost (1 Cor.16:8), which usually fell at the last of May. There are no reasons to believe Paul drastically changed his plans even though a peaceful departure from Ephesus was changed by an uproar over him (Acts 19:23-41). When the uproar was over, Paul bade the disciples farewell and proceeded according to plan through Macedonia to Corinth, where he remained three months for the winter (Acts 20:1-3). After winter, he journeyed toward Jerusalem passing through Macedonia again (Acts 20:3). Paul left Philippi after the days of unleavened bread (Acts 20:6), probably in mid-April, and reached his destination at Jerusalem, apparently near Pentecost as planned (Acts 20:16). The journey from Ephesus to Jerusalem lasted one full year. When we add the years spent at Ephesus and his travel time from Antioch to Ephesus, the *third* missionary journey took a total of five years. This places Paul's entry into Jerusalem in May, 58 A.D.

58-65 A.D.

Paul had been in Jerusalem only seven days when he was mobbed by the Jews (Acts 21:27). He was rescued from the murderous hands of the Jews by the Roman captain, Claudius Lysias. He was later arrested and sent to Caesarea. Five days later, Paul made his defense before Felix, governor of Judea (Acts 21:33; cf.24:11). This appearance before Felix took place around the first of June in 58 A.D. Felix deferred action commanding that Paul be kept prisoner. Paul remained a prisoner in Caesarea for two years (Acts 24:27) at which time Festus replaced Felix as governor in the late spring of 60 A.D. Shortly thereafter, Paul appeared before Festus, who honored his appeal to Caesar's court (Acts 25:11). After an appearance before King Agrippa II later that year (Acts 25:23-32), Paul was sent to Rome.

The journey to Rome took between five and six months (cf.Acts 27:2-5,7,20,27,33; 28:11-14). Leaving Caesarea the last of October or the first of November, 60 A.D., he arrived in Rome the last of March or the first of April, 61 A.D. Here, Paul was a prisoner of the Roman state and kept under house arrest (Acts 28:16). He remained in Rome as a prisoner for two whole years (Acts 28:30), or until the spring of 63 A.D.

Luke's account of the life and travels of Paul, as recorded in the book of Acts, ends in the spring of 63 A.D. This does not mean, however, that the activities of Paul ended then. The epistles written by Paul while a prisoner in Rome indicates anticipation of being freed. They also infer plans to visit places he had not visited previously, e.g., Colosse (Phile.22; cf.Col.4:7-9), and to revisit places he visited earlier, e.g., Jerusalem (Heb.13:23,24) and Philippi (Phil.1:23-26; 2:23,24). In addition, Paul wrote two epistles to Timothy and one to Titus that could not have been written prior to 63 A.D. The circumstances surrounding these epistles did not exist prior to 63. Furthermore, Paul mentioned visiting places the circumstances of which did not develop prior to 63 A.D. Therefore, we believe Paul was released from prison and did indeed carry out his wishes and plans of travel after 63 A.D. In the process of discussing the epistles written from Rome and those written after 63 A.D., we shall seek to unfold what appears to have been the course of those travels.

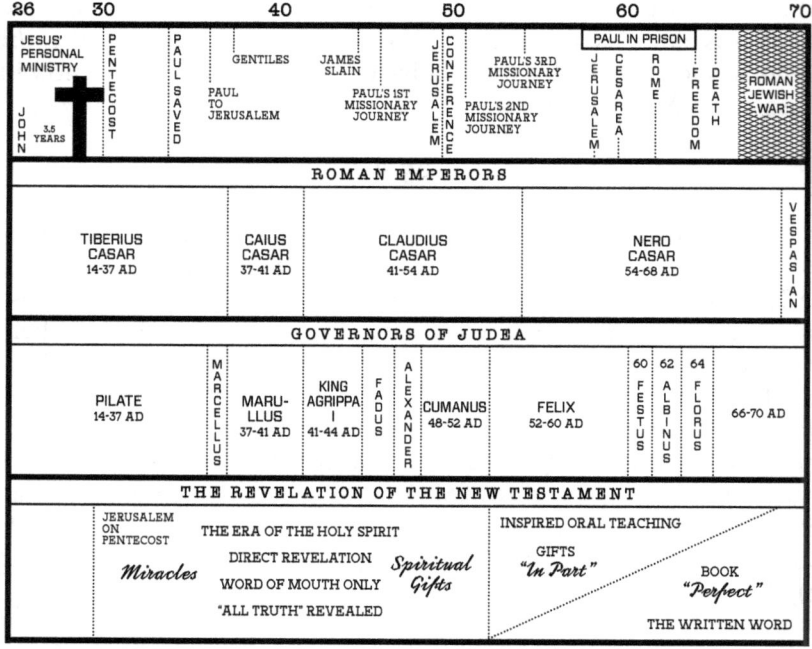

The above chart is available at the front of the book in a larger format and will be useful in following the highlights of the history of Christianity through these years as they relate to the corresponding secular history of the times. It will also be useful in our continued discussion of the development of the New Testament. The reader may wish to refer to it frequently.

Lesson Exercises

Fill In The Blank

1. The second missionary journey of Paul began at _____ _____ (Acts 15:40,41).

2. Paul took with him _____ on this journey.

3. They passed through _____ and _____ confirming the churches.

4. _____ joined Paul at Lystra and _____ joined them at Troas.

5. Paul preached first in Europe at _____.

6. The households of _____ and the _____ were converted at Philippi.

7. Paul left _____ at Philippi and he, Timothy and Silas went to Thessalonica.

8. Most of Paul's time on the second missionary journey was spent in _____.

9. Paul came in contact with _____ and _____ in Corinth who became faithful co-workers.

10. Paul went to _____ when his work in Corinth ended.

True or False

1. _____ Paul went up to Antioch to observe the Passover.

2. _____ Paul's third missionary journey began at Antioch.

3. _____ John the Baptist baptized 12 disciples in Ephesus.

4. _____ Paul taught for two years in the school of Tyrannus.

5. _____ Paul planned to spend the winter of 57 A.D. in Corinth.

6. _____ Paul carried contributions from churches to the saints in Jerusalem.

7. _____ Paul stopped at Troas on his way to Jerusalem.

8. _____ Paul hoped to arrive in Jerusalem in time for Passover.

9. _____ Pilate rescued Paul from a Jewish mob in Jerusalem.

10. _____ Paul appeared before governors and kings in Caesarea.

Match

1. Luke
2. Timothy
3. Corinth
4. Athens
5. Acquila & Priscilla
6. Ephesus
7. Claudius Lysias
8. Felix
9. Colossians
10. 2 Timothy

_____ Mars Hill
_____ School of Tyrannus
_____ Governor of Judea
_____ Written from Rome
_____ 18 months, Acts 18:11
_____ Paul's last epistle
_____ The Physician
_____ Roman Captain
_____ A young man
_____ Tent makers

Questions

1. What two things did Paul and Silas seek to accomplish in Syria and Cilicia on the second missionary journey (cf.Acts 15:40,41)?

2. Where did Paul envision a man calling him to come to Macedonia?

3. Why were Paul and Silas cast into prison at Philippi?

4. Who troubled Paul most in Thessalonica and Berea?

5. To what cities of Greece (Achaia) did Paul go alone?

6. Why were Acquila and Priscilla in Corinth?

7. What regions did Paul first cover on his third missionary journey (Acts 18:23)?

8. How long did Paul stay in Ephesus (Acts 20:31)?

9. What happened in Ephesus before Paul left there (Acts 19)?

10. Why was Paul mobbed in Jerusalem (Acts 21:26-40)?

Notes

LESSON 05

THE PRIMARY & LITERARY REVELATION

Our Purpose Restated

In the two previous lessons, we reconstructed the history of the first forty years of Christianity. Let us now return to the questions raised earlier in this study: (1) Did the Holy Spirit fully accomplish His work in guiding the apostles into *all truth?* (2) If so, at what point in history was this work completed? Let us answer these questions from two viewpoints: (1) the Spirit's primary revelation and (2) the Spirit's literary revelation of the New Testament.

The Primary Revelation

The Holy Spirit first came on Pentecost endowing the apostles so that they spoke *"as the Spirit gave them utterance"* (Acts 2:4). Wherever they witnessed thereafter, it was by the power of the Holy Spirit directing them (Acts 2:33; 4:31; 5:32). All of the New Testament order was not revealed on Pentecost, however, nor in the days immediately following. The acceptability of the Gentiles was not fully understood until the conversion of the household of Cornelius (Acts 10), which did not occur until between 37-39 A.D. The disciples were not given their new name (cf.Isa.62:1,2) until 43 A.D. where, in Antioch, they were first *"called Christians"* (Acts 11:26). Therefore, thirteen years after Pentecost additional truth was still being revealed.

In 49 or 50 A.D. a matter arose that put the Holy Spirit on trial regarding the accomplishing of His purpose. Paul and Barnabas were converting Gentiles, but the Holy Spirit had not instructed them to command the Gentiles to be circumcised and to keep the Law of Moses. There were men, however, who went to Antioch from Judea teaching that Gentiles must be circumcised and keep the Law (Acts 15:1,5,24). *"No small dissension and debate"* arose over the matter. Obviously if the other apostles preached this doctrine under the power of the Holy Spirit, while Paul and Barnabas had not been similarly instructed, then something was wrong—basically wrong—and had to be settled! The Holy Spirit cannot contradict Himself (1 Jn.2:20,21). So, Paul and Barnabas went up to Jerusalem *"because of a revelation"* (Gal.2:2), i.e., directed by the Holy Spirit. There the debate continued. The conclusion of all the apostles was that the Holy Spirit had not authorized these

Judaizers so to speak (Acts 15:6-21). An epistle was drafted to be sent to the brethren who were of the Gentiles in Antioch, Syria and Cilicia signifying that the Judaizers taught without authority (Acts 15:14,28). This letter contained the declarations of the apostles, elders and *Holy Spirit* concerning these men. It contained the revelation of *truth* not previously made known. This indicated the Holy Spirit's *continuing* work in the revelation of *all truth* began on Pentecost (Acts 2).

As far as we can determine, there was no additional revelation of *new truth* by the Holy Spirit *after* the "Jerusalem Conference," A.D. 49 or 50. Either at this point, or shortly thereafter, *"faith that was once for all delivered to the saints."* was completely revealed (Jude 3). In 58 A.D. Paul said to the Ephesian elders, *"I did not shrink from declaring to you anything that was profitable... for I did not shrink from declaring to you the whole counsel of God... In all things I have shown you..."* (Acts 20:20,27,35). Within eight years of the Jerusalem Conference *"the whole counsel of God"* had been revealed. In fact, not later than five and one-half years after the conference, Paul instructed the Galatians to refuse the acceptance of teachers preaching *"any other gospel"* than that which they had received (Gal.1:8,9 KJV). This declaration precluded the acceptance of additional revelations of new truth. The churches of Galatia had received *"the decisions"* of the Jerusalem Conference within a year, as Paul began his *second* missionary journey (Acts 16:1-6). These facts tend to suggest that the Holy Spirit completed His work of revealing *"all truth"* by the end of the conference, not later than 50 A.D.

It further appears to this student that a portion of the "Conference Letter" indicated the end of the revelation of new truth. The letter said, *"For it has seemed good to the Holy Spirit and to us to lay on you no greater burden than these requirements"* (Acts 15:28). The conference gathered to consider whether circumcision and the keeping of the Law of Moses were requirements upon the Gentiles. They refused to bind the Law upon Gentile Christians, and bound upon them only the additional *"requirements"* of abstaining from meats offered to idols, blood, things strangled and fornication. We need to understand that these things were not added from the Law of Moses, but were rather incorporated as part of the New Covenant. The statement of verse 28 must be understood, not as an addition to the gospel from the Law of Moses but as requirements of the *"Law of Christ"* (Gal.5:14)! This being the case, the statement, *"For it has seemed good to the Holy Spirit and to us to lay on you no greater burden than these requirements"* (*"these necessary things,"* KJV), precluded the future addition of new burdens by further revelations of new requirements. Otherwise, this statement (Acts 15:28) is false.

The Holy Spirit finished His primary work of revelation concluding it by the end of the Jerusalem conference (49 or 50 A.D.). Until this time, *not one word* of the New Testament had been written! It is interesting to note that at the very instant the Holy Spirit finished His work of guiding the apostles into all truth, He began guiding the writing of the New Testament. The conference epistle constitutes the first inspired words of the New Testament scriptures penned!

The Literary Revelation

The inspired Word of God during the first twenty years came through the spoken word of inspired men. The epistle written by all the apostles and elders at Jerusalem changed that. No doubt the inspired words of the apostles were sufficient to convince the Jewish Christians relative to their attitude toward their Gentile counterparts. The inspired epistle accomplished more than that. It served to open the door to the acceptability of the procession of epistles that followed. The inspired epistle was as authoritative as the inspired man and was delivered as such to the churches (Acts 15:30; 16:4,5). The written word, then, was of equal authority with the spoken word. Since the revelation of all truth was completed prior to the writing of any of it, the written word could not contain anything that had not already been revealed! The written word, of necessity, had to conform to the spoken word or else the Holy Spirit had not guided the apostles into all truth.[22]

In discussing spiritual gifts, Paul said, *"Love never ends. As for prophecies, they will pass away; as for tongues, they will cease; as for knowledge, it will pass away. For we know in part and we prophesy in part, but when the perfect comes, the partial will pass away"* (1 Cor.13:8-10). The Holy Spirit, by way of spiritual gifts, provided the complete revelation of the truth to the early Christians in fragmentary portions. Apart from the apostles, all of the truth was not contained in any one man. While the early disciples had all the truth revealed by the apostles and made available through spiritual gifts, they could not put them all together and observe the complete package of truth. The gifts were serving their purpose for the time present, but the church could not come to maturity and completeness until *"the perfect comes."* This word *"perfect" (teleios)* signifies completeness and suggests the completion of the written word.[23] In the infant stage of Christianity spiritual gifts were essential to the maturing process until the written word brought them to full maturity. But Paul said that *"when the perfect comes,"* the childish things would be put away (1 Cor.13:11-13), the prophecies would fail, the tongues would cease and inspired knowledge would vanish (1 Cor.13:8).

These words were penned when only three of the New Testament books were in existence. Twenty-four books remained to be written, which means the spiritual gifts were still very much at work and remained at work until the completion of the written New Testament. Let us now observe the development of the New Testament scriptures book by book.

1 Thessalonians (52 A.D.)

The *first* book of the New Testament to be written was 1 Thessalonians. It was written by Paul (1 Thess.1:1), probably in late 52 A.D., while at Corinth. The church at Thessalonica was established by Paul, Silas and Timothy in 51 A.D. after they left Philippi (Acts 17:1-9). It appears that only a short time, perhaps a month or so, was spent by Paul in Thessalonica before disturbances forced his leaving. After approximately the same amount of time in Berea (Acts 17:10-15), Paul went to Athens where he spent at least one month. Timothy, who joined Paul at Athens approximately two or more weeks after the apostle arrived (Acts 17:15), was sent to Thessalonica from Athens (1 Thess.3:1-6). Shortly after Timothy returned to Thessalonica from Athens, Paul went to Corinth (Acts 18:1), where Timothy returned to him from Thessalonica (Acts 18:5). We do not know how long Timothy was separated from Paul, but the church at Thessalonica existed long enough when Paul wrote this epistle to have elders (1 Thess.5:12) and a broad influence throughout Macedonia and Achaia (1 Thess.1:6-8). We suggest that this epistle was written in the latter part of 52 A.D., at least one year after the church at Thessalonica was established.

The *first* book of our New Testament to be written conforms to the principles already demanded by our conclusions in this study. It also establishes the fundamental rules which resulted in the development, reproduction and preservation of all New Testament scripture. First, there is nothing contained in this book that constitutes **new doctrine** to the Thessalonians. It contains only what they had been taught earlier. Notice Paul's statement: *"Now concerning brotherly love you have no need for anyone to write to you, for you yourselves have been taught by God to love one another"* (1 Thess.4:9). Again, *"now concerning the times and the seasons, brothers, you have no need to have anything written to you. For you yourselves are fully aware that the day of the Lord will come like a thief in the night"* (1 Thess.5:1,2). How were they *"taught by God"* so they would be *"fully aware"* of those things? Many of them had been endowed with the Holy Spirit by the laying on of the apostle's hands and, therefore, knew all things (cf.1 Thess.4:8; 5:19; 2 Thess.2:2). Secondly, there are principles within this book establishing its future and universal authority. Paul said, *"I charge you by the Lord that this epistle be read unto all the holy brethren"* (1 Thess.5:27 KJV). These were not just the holy brethren at Thessalonica, even though this epistle was addressed to them. Rather, this charge was directed toward making this epistle available to all the holy brethren throughout the world! The Thessalonians obviously understood this charge because holy brethren throughout the world are still reading it. This charge established the rule by which all the New Testament books were written, reproduced and preserved for all generations.

Lesson Exercises

Questions

1. What important truth was challenged by the presence of Judaizers at Antioch?

2. What motivated Paul and Barnabas to go up to Jerusalem (cf.Gal.2:2)?

3. Were the apostles, elders and Holy Spirit united?

4. What part of the epistle (Acts 15:23-29) indicates all truth had been revealed to the apostles?

5. Would there be any revelation of new truth after the conference?

6. When did the writing of the New Testament begin?

7. Was there a period of time when both inspired men and epistles were authoritative?

8. Did the time come when there was only the inspired book? Explain:

9. Do we have inspired men today? If not, why not?

10. How can we determine the false teachers of our day?

Lesson 05 - The Primary and Literary Revelation

True or False

1. _____ The Holy Spirit came upon people to show they were saved.

2. _____ What Paul taught he learned from the Apostles.

3. _____ The Judaizing teachers taught the truth because they were inspired.

4. _____ Peter and Paul found themselves in conflict at the Jerusalem conference.

5. _____ Paul was not as inspired as the other apostles.

6. _____ When that which was perfect came, that which was in part was done away.

7. _____ 1 Thessalonians was written by Paul from Corinth.

8. _____ The church at Thessalonica was started by Paul, Silas and Timothy.

9. _____ The church at Thessalonica had not received all of the truth.

10. _____ The church at Thessalonica was instructed to share their epistle.

Match

1. Galatians 1:6-9   _____ Conversion of Cornelius
2. Jude 3   _____ A new name
3. Acts 20:27   _____ The promise of Holy Spirit
4. Isaiah 62:1,2   _____ Distort the gospel
5. Acts 15:23-29   _____ Know all things
6. Acts 11:26   _____ The faith once for all delivered
7. Acts 5:32   _____ Conference epistle
8. Acts 10   _____ Christians
9. 1 John 2:20,21   _____ The whole counsel
10. Acts 2:33   _____ The Holy Spirit's witness

Fill In The Blank

1. The Gentiles were first converted at the household of _____.

2. The disciples were called _____ first in Antioch (Acts 11:26).

3. Paul kept back _____ profitable but declared the _____ _____ of God to the Ephesians and showed them _____ _____ (Acts 20:20,27,35).

4. The Galatians were warned against preachers who preached a _____ gospel.

5. The Jerusalem conference was conducted around the year _____A.D.

6. The first part of our New Testament to be written was the _____ epistle.

7. The first book of the New Testament to be written was _____ _____.

8. Paul wrote 1 Thessalonians while at _____.

9. Before the inspired book, God's word was in the inspired _____.

10. The New Testament order was _____ revealed before it was written.

LESSON 06

THE LITERARY REVELATION CONTINUES

We began our study of the New Testament books as they developed. First Thessalonians was the first book of our New Testament penned. As we continue, we shall look for the date and place of writing of each book. We shall also observe whether or not the New Testament books contain any revelation of truth not previously revealed.

2 Thessalonians (53 A.D.)

The second book of the New Testament to be written was 2 Thessalonians. It was written from Corinth a few months after the first epistle, probably in the early part of 53 A.D. The book was written while Paul, Silas and Timothy were still together (2 Thess.1:1). The last place they are mentioned as being together was at Corinth (2 Cor.1:19). Paul left Corinth for Ephesus and Jerusalem in the spring of 53 A.D. (Acts 18:18-21).

This epistle, like the first, contains no new teaching. After declaring unto them an astounding bit of information about the *"rebellion"* and the revealing of *"the man of lawlessness"* (2 Thess.2:3), Paul wrote, *"Do you not remember that when I was still with you I told you these things?"* (2 Thess.2:5). So, the commandments of the epistle were simply a restatement of the law of Christ already revealed orally.

Furthermore, Paul forcefully acknowledged the authority of this epistle. First, he placed it on equal par with the spoken word: *"So then, brothers, stand firm and hold to the traditions that you were taught by us, either by our spoken word or by our letter"* (2 Thess.2:15). Second, he proclaimed, *"If anyone does not obey what we say in this letter, take note of that person, and have nothing to do with him, that he may be ashamed"* (2 Thess.3:14). The authority of the written word, then, is equal to the authority of the spoken word.

Galatians (55 or 56 A.D.)

Galatians was the third book of our New Testament written. It was composed by Paul (Gal.1:1), probably in 55 A.D. while he was at Ephesus. Paul's *first* missionary journey took him into the regions of

Asia Minor identified by Luke as Pamphylia, Pisidia and Lycaonia (Acts 13:13,14; 14:6). These sections also constituted the southern portion of the Roman Province known as *Galatia*.[24] Paul and Barnabas established the churches of Galatia on this journey. Two years later, following the Jerusalem Conference, Paul again visited them, confirming them (Acts 15:41) and delivering unto them *"the decisions"* resulting from the Jerusalem Conference (Acts 16:4,6). He then passed into Europe on his *second* missionary journey and, after three years, returned to Galatia as he journeyed to Ephesus on his *third* missionary journey (Acts 18:23). The historian, Luke, never indicated problems among the Galatians on any of these visits. It is assumed, therefore, that problems arose sometime after Paul's visit in 54 A.D. Paul indicates the problems suddenly surfaced and he was astonished by them (Gal.1:6). The most probable time for such a reaction would have been after his visit with them in 54 A.D. We envision Titus, an uncircumcised Greek (Gal.2:1), who was with Paul in Ephesus early in 56 A.D. (cf.2 Cor.8:6,10,16,23; 9:2; 12:18), visiting and being rejected by the churches of Galatia in 55 A.D., and then bringing the report of their departure from the truth to Paul at Ephesus. This would explain Paul's astonishment at them *"so quickly deserting"* (Gal.1:6) when earlier they *"were running well"* (Gal.5:7). It also explains why Paul took special pains to prove to the Galatians that Titus, his proof case, was accepted by all the apostles at Jerusalem (Gal.2:1-9) without circumcision. Upon hearing of their departure from the truth, Paul wrote this epistle to correct it.

Other dates have been advanced. Some contend that the book was written in 50 A.D. from Antioch. Others contend that it was written in 52 A.D. from Corinth and others in 57 A.D. from Macedonia. Each of these dates, in some ways, meet the requirements demanded by the nature of the book and its contents. It appears to this student, however, that the date we have advocated is the most reasonable for the following reasons: (1) Paul acknowledges being in contact with the Galatians during this time, 55 or 56 A.D. (1 Cor.16:1). (2) Titus was Paul's test case regarding circumcision (Gal.2:1,3). He was with Paul during this time and sent by Paul to Corinth to accomplish in the Corinthians the same work (the ministering to the poor saints at Jerusalem, 2 Cor.8:6,10,23; 9:2; 12:18) he sought to accomplish with the Galatians (1 Cor.16:1). The presence of Titus in Ephesus in 56 A.D. would have provided the perfect explanation of the Galatian problem. (3) The absence of any hint of Paul planning a future visit to Galatia (cf.Gal.4:20) would indicate the epistle was written after Paul's *third* visit with them in 54 A.D. (Acts 18:23). (4) The fact that the Galatians were *"so quickly deserting"* unto another gospel (Gal.1:6) suggests a rapid departure. The date of 55 or 56 A.D. at Ephesus would satisfy all of the demands of the epistle relative to time and place.

The book of Galatians, like the two Thessalonian epistles, contains no *new teaching*. The Galatians knew the truth (Gal.3:1; 5:7). Paul said to them, *"But even if we or an angel from heaven should preach to you a gospel contrary to the one we preached to you, let him be accursed. As we have said before, so now I say again: If anyone is preaching to you a gospel contrary to the one you received, let him be accursed"* (Gal.1:8,9). This passage relates three facts that need to be impressed in our study. First, there was not to be any additional revelation of *truth* to the Galatians. They had already received *"all the truth"* (Jn.16:13). Consequently, even this epistle could not contain any new revelation of truth without an anathema of God upon Paul. They had already received the complete revelation. Second, the Galatian letter of necessity had to be written after the Jerusalem Conference because the *conference letter* contained what appears to be new revelation. Third, no new truth was to be revealed, even by an angel. This is significant for the book of Revelation was revealed by an angel (Rev.1:1; 22:6). This fact demands that whatever truth was revealed by the angel to John in the Apocalypse be already revealed by word of mouth long before it was penned on Patmos. This fact alone destroys the demands of so-called scholarship that the Apocalypse contains doctrines not related prior to its writings, and that its teaching demands a late date. The fact is, the *truth of the New Testament had all been revealed before any of it was written!*

1 Corinthians (57 A.D.)

The first Corinthian letter was the fourth book of our New Testament penned. Paul had been in Ephesus since the late spring of 54 A.D. Sometime in 57 A.D., as the winter subsided, Paul made plans to leave Ephesus for Macedonia and Achaia to revisit the churches and then go on to Jerusalem (Acts 19:21). With these plans formulated, he sent Timothy and Erastus into Macedonia (Acts 19:22) with the expectation that Timothy would go as far as Corinth (cf.1 Cor.4:17). Paul remained in Asia for a season (Acts 19:22) planning to leave Ephesus after Pentecost, the last of May (1 Cor.16:8). While he tarried, some brethren from Corinth came to Paul asking certain questions (1 Cor.1:11; 7:1; 16:17). Paul answered by writing this epistle in the early spring of 57 A.D. in response to their coming and the church's immediate need.

We call this epistle *"The First Epistle to the Corinthians,"* but it is actually Paul's second epistle to them (cf.1 Cor.5:9-11; 2 Cor.13:1,2,10). A year prior to this epistle, Paul wrote to them in which, among other things, he discussed the contribution for the saints at Jerusalem (1 Cor.16:1,2; cf.2 Cor.8:10; 9:2). It appears that Titus, who came to Paul at Ephesus, was persuaded by Paul to go to Corinth for the purpose of instructing the church and preparing them for this ministry (2 Cor.8:6,16,17,23; 12:18). This was the occasion for the delivery of the first epistle Paul had written a few months earlier. This epistle was not preserved for us.

The first Corinthian letter, like the others, contained only such teaching as that already preached to them by word of mouth. Through spiritual gifts (1 Cor.12:1-11), the Corinthians had received the fullness of the revelation. Paul said to them, *"that in every way you were enriched in him in all speech and all knowledge— even as the testimony about Christ was confirmed among you— so that you are not lacking in any gift, as you wait for the revealing of our Lord Jesus Christ"* (1 Cor.1:5-7). Again, he said, *"That is why I sent you Timothy, my beloved and faithful child in the Lord, to remind you of my ways in Christ, as I teach them everywhere in every church"* (1 Cor.4:17). Notice that Timothy could only bring to their remembrance the things they had already been taught. Again, *"We have the mind of Christ"* (1 Cor.2:16). Therefore, what Paul wrote in this epistle was not new doctrine. Furthermore, it was authoritative. The epistle contained *"a command of the Lord"* (1 Cor.14:37) designed for universal application (1 Cor.1:2) so that the revealed word of God by this epistle is of divine authority for all times.

2 Corinthians (57 A.D.)

The second epistle to the Corinthians was written by Paul from Macedonia, probably at Philippi, in the late summer or early fall of 57 A.D. After Paul left Ephesus in the spring of 57 A.D. (Acts 20:1), he went to Troas where he waited for Titus to come from Corinth (2 Cor.2:12,13). While Paul was at Troas, a great door of opportunity opened for him and, apparently, the church was established. Paul's previous visit to Troas (Acts 16:8-11) was only the stop he made before being called to go into Macedonia. This would explain why he made it a point to journey through there on his way from Macedonia to Jerusalem (Acts 20:3-6). After a short time there, Paul took leave and went into Macedonia (2 Cor.2:13) where Titus came to him (2 Cor.7:5-7). This became the occasion for the writing of the second epistle to the Corinthians as Titus went back to Achaia and Corinth to complete the collection for the saints at Jerusalem (2 Cor.8:6,16-18,22-24). Within a reasonable period of time, Paul followed Titus and the letter to Corinth where he spent the winter (Acts 20:2,3).

Paul's purpose in this epistle, again, was not to reveal new truth unto the Corinthians. The purpose as stated by Paul was to *"test you and know whether you are obedient in everything"* (2 Cor.2:9). Again, he said, *"This is the third time I am coming to you. Every charge must be established by the evidence of two or three witnesses. I warned those who sinned before and all the others, and I warn them now while absent, as I did when present on my second visit, that if I come again I will not spare them—since you seek proof that Christ is speaking in me. He is not weak in dealing with you, but is powerful among you... For this reason I write these things while I am away from you, that when I come I may not have to be severe in my use of the authority that the Lord has given me for building up and not for tearing down"* (2 Cor.13:1-3,10). These texts demonstrate that the authority of Paul's pen was as forceful as the authority of his speech. Yet, it must be remembered that the words written were not different from the words spoken while he was with them. He said, *"For we are not writing to you anything other than what you read and understand and I hope you will fully understand"* (2 Cor.1:13). So, this epistle likewise establishes the premise that the New Testament law was fully revealed *before* any of it was written.

Romans (58 A.D.)

The next book of the New Testament written was the book of Romans. It was written by Paul (Rom.1:1) from Corinth early in 58 A.D., probably in January or February. Paul's plans were to winter in Corinth (1 Cor.16:6). Apparently, he did so in the home of Gaius (Rom.16:23; cf.1 Cor.1:14). At the time of this writing, the contributions of Macedonia and Achaia for the poor saints at Jerusalem were ready for delivery and Paul was ready to go to Jerusalem with them (Rom.15:25,26). Since Paul left Achaia early enough to be in Philippi of Macedonia by Passover (Acts 20:6), which came the first of April, the epistle had to be written prior to the middle of March. The journey to Philippi alone would have taken approximately two weeks.

Again, Paul's purpose in writing this epistle was not to teach new revelation. He said to them, *"I myself am satisfied about you, my brothers, that you yourselves are full of goodness, filled with all knowledge and able to instruct one another"* (Rom.15:14). The Roman Christians were *"by the power of the Holy Spirit"* Where did they get it? Answer: *"by the power of the Holy Spirit"* (Rom.15:13). *"But on some points I have written to you very boldly by way of reminder, because of the grace given me by God"* (Rom.15:15). Paul wrote them *"by way of reminder,"* or to put them *"in mind"* (KJV). His purpose, then, in writing to the Romans was not to reveal new truth but to remind them of what they already knew.

Lesson Exercises

True or False

1. _____ The last place Paul, Silas and Timothy are mentioned as being together was at Corinth.
2. _____ All of the N.T. books contain doctrines never before revealed.
3. _____ The written word is not as authoritative as the spoken word.
4. _____ The book of Acts was written by a physician named Luke.
5. _____ Titus was a Jew.
6. _____ The book of Revelation cannot be trusted because it was revealed by an angel.
7. _____ Paul sent Timothy and Erastus from Ephesus into Macedonia (Acts 19:22).
8. _____ Titus delivered the first letter to the Corinthians (2 Cor.8:6,16,17,23; 12:18).
9. _____ Paul may have established the church at Troas after leaving Ephesus.
10. _____ Paul was a guest of Erastus while in Corinth (Rom.16:23; 1 Cor.1:14).

Fill In The Blank

1. The Gentiles were first converted at the household of _____.

2. "So then, brothers, stand firm and hold to the _____ that you were taught by us, either by our _____ _____, or by our _____" (2 Thess.2:15).

3. "That in every way you were enriched in him in all _____ and all _____" (1 Cor.1:5).

4. "That is why I sent you Timothy... to _____ you of my ways in Christ, as I teach them everywhere in every church" (1 Cor.4:17).

5. "If anyone thinks that he is a prophet, or spiritual, he should acknowledge that the things I am writing to you are a _____ of the Lord" (1 Cor.14:37).

6. "For we are not writing to you anything other than what you _____ and _____ and I hope you will fully _____" (2 Cor.1:13).

7. "I myself am satisfied about you... that you yourselves are ... filled with all _____" (Rom.15:14).

Questions

1. Who was with Paul when he wrote 2 Thessalonians?

2. When did Paul leave Corinth?

3. What would cause anyone to believe Paul wrote Galatians from Ephesus?

4. What noted evangelist did Paul not compel to be circumcised (Gal.2:3)?

5. Could the Galatians receive any new revelations after Paul's epistle to them?

6. Do we have any examples of Angels revealing God's truth?

7. Why did Paul write 1 Corinthians?

8. Was the 1 Corinthian letter Paul's first epistle to them?

9. Where did Paul wait for Titus to come to him from Corinth?

10. Why was Paul in Corinth when he wrote the book of Romans?

Match

1. First book written
2. Second book written
3. Third book written
4. Fourth book written
5. Fifth book written
6. Sixth book written
7. 2 Thessalonians
8. 1 Corinthians
9. 2 Corinthians
10. Galatians

____ 2 Corinthians
____ Written from Corinth
____ 2 Thessalonians
____ Romans
____ Written from Ephesus
____ 1 Thessalonians
____ Written from Macedonia
____ Probably written at Ephesus
____ 1 Corinthians
____ Galatians

LESSON 07

PAUL'S LITERARY INTERLUDE

Between 52 and 58 A.D., Paul wrote six of our New Testament books. During the next four years, however, his pen is noticeably silent. These were the years of travel and imprisonment at Caesarea and Rome (58-63 A.D.). While Paul was active in teaching during this period, he did not return to dictating epistles until his last year in Rome. This does not mean there were no books written during this interlude. It is rather certain that the gospel of Luke and the epistle of James were written during this time. Luke indicates the possibility that other gospel accounts were also written during this period. He said, *"Inasmuch as many have undertaken to compile a narrative of the things that have been accomplished among us, just as those who from the beginning were eyewitnesses and ministers of the word have delivered them to us, it seemed good to me also...to write an orderly account for you..."* (Lk.1:1-3). It is altogether possible the books of Matthew, Mark and even John were written prior to Luke's account.

Determining the date and authorship of the four Gospels is a very difficult problem. They are biographical in nature, dealing with Christ's personal ministry (26-30 A.D.), and were written no less than twenty-five years after the time period which they cover. Clues relative to their authorship and date of writing are very scarce. The student must bear this in mind, particularly in relation to the writings of Matthew and Mark where the clues are very, very few and inconclusive.

Matthew (55-63 A.D.?)

Many think the gospel according to Matthew was the first of the four gospels written. Since Luke's gospel was written sometime between 58 and 63 A.D., Matthew's account of the life of Christ must precede that time period. Varying conservative scholars have dated it anywhere from 55 to 63 A.D. There is nothing within the book, however, that contributes to an understanding of the matter. Tradition, which is always weak and unreliable, testifies to the early date.[25]

Whether or not Matthew wrote the gospel which bears his name is not known. The earliest traditions attribute it to him but, again, this is circumstantial. If the apostle Matthew wrote it, the nearest he came to identifying himself is (1) his use of his name *"Matthew"* (Matt.9:9) instead of *"Levi"* as used by Mark (Mk.2:14) and Luke (Lk.5:27), (2) his refusal to identify himself as the host of Jesus for a meal (Matt.9:10-13; cf.Mk.2:15-17; Lk.5:29-32), and (3) his specific identification of his own profession, *"tax collector"* (Matt.10:3), in his apostolic list in which he fails to identify the occupation of the others. These clues are not sufficiently strong of themselves to identify Matthew as the author, but they do fall within the same vein of evidence that characterizes all four gospel accounts.

The credibility and authority of this book is established in two ways. It is first established by the perfect harmony of its subject matter with the other three gospel accounts. This testifies to the correctness of its content. Second, a portion of its content is quoted by Paul as Scripture. In 1 Timothy 5:18, Paul said, *"For the Scripture says, ... The laborer deserves his wages."* Since this quotation appears only in the New Testament (cf.Matt.10:10; Lk.10:7), it identifies the books where it is found as Scripture. *"All Scripture is breathed out by God"* (2 Tim.3:16), therefore, the gospel according to Matthew occupies its rightful place in our New Testament scriptures.

Mark (60-61 A.D.?)

Many conservative scholars feel that Mark penned the first gospel record while others feel that he was second. The clues generally relied upon for such information are missing in the work, and there is nothing to instruct us. The exact date of its writing cannot be determined. We place his gospel in this time frame mainly because Luke indicated that more than one account of the life of Christ had been written prior to his own account (Lk.1:1-3).

It is likewise impossible to determine the author of the book with any certainty. Tradition has generally attributed it to John Mark, the nephew of Barnabas (Col.4:10; Acts 12:12), who accompanied Paul and Barnabas on their *first* missionary journey but turned back at Perga in Pamphylia (Acts 13:13). This act of immaturity became a source of contention between Paul and Barnabas, resulting in their separating for the *second* missionary journey (Acts 15:36-39). Mark finally demonstrated his fidelity and became a useful co-laborer for a while with Paul (cf.Phile.24; Col.4:10; 2 Tim.4:11). Mark was also an assistant of the apostle Peter in Babylon (1 Pet.5:13). If Mark wrote the book, he saw fit, perhaps, to convey only one small bit of information concerning himself. On the night on which Jesus was betrayed, when all of His disciples had forsaken him, *"a young man followed him, with nothing but a linen cloth about his body. And they seized him, but he left the linen cloth and ran away naked"* (Mk.14:51,52). The account serves no purpose contextually. Since the home of John Mark was in Jerusalem (Acts 12:12), and he would have been a young lad about this time, we reason that he might be the person described. Perhaps, as John's identification appears in the expression *"the disciple whom Jesus loved"* (Jn.21:20-24), Mark's identification is seen in his portrayal of the lad who lost his wrap and fled nude at the arrest of Jesus. Mark's gospel alone reveals this story.

James (60-62 A.D.?)

The book of James evidently fits into this time period also. Its author is *"James, a servant of God and of the Lord Jesus Christ"* (Jas.1:1). There are three different men in the New Testament identified by this name: (1) James, the son of Zebedee, who was the first apostle martyred (Acts 12:1,2); (2) James, the son of Alpheus, whose activities are not detailed in the New Testament; and (3) James, the Lord's brother, who seems to have been one of the elders of the church in Jerusalem (cf. Acts 15:13; 21:18; Gal.1:19; 2:9,12). The book of James could not have been written by the son of Zebedee because he was dead before the conditions described in the book developed. Some scholars believe the other two were the same person but, in either case, the consensus is that the book was written by the James identified as the Lord's brother.

The exact date of the book of James cannot be determined. It addresses the Jews of *"the dispersion,"* i.e., those Jews scattered into the various countries of the world. This fact alone excludes the son of Zebedee as author. In 44 A.D., when James was slain, the gospel had not been preached to all the Jews of the dispersion. Furthermore, at the time of its writing, the revelation of *all truth* was complete and was identified as *"the perfect law, the law of liberty"* (Jas.1:25). This demands a date after 50 A.D., for the Jerusalem Conference convened to determine a point of law. The bigger part of the evangelization of the Jews of the dispersion was not complete until at least 58 A.D. It would appear the epistle was written after this period of time.

James, the brother of the Lord, was put to death by Ananus, the High Priest, shortly after the death of Festus in 62 A.D. This probably occurred late in 62, or early 63 A.D.[26] It appears from chapter 5 that James was pronouncing doom upon the persecutors of the Jewish Christians (Jas.5:1-6) and calling upon the faithful to be patient, *"until the coming of the Lord*" (Jas.5:7-9). The obvious reference is not to the final coming of the Lord, but to His coming in judgment upon the Jewish persecutors of God's faithful people. The epistle seems to fall into the time period when the Christians were being prepared for the great period of suffering promised upon the world (cf.Acts 13:40,41; 1 Thess.2:14-16; Heb.10:32-37; Lk.21:12-19). It further reflects a similar attitude as that expressed by James when Paul arrived at Jerusalem in 58 A.D. (Acts 21:20-22). We would date the book no earlier than 60 A.D., and no later than early 62 A.D.

The book contains no new doctrine. James recognized only one *"lawgiver"* (Jas.4:12) who revealed *"the perfect law, the law of liberty"* (Jas.1:25). Perfect (*teleios*)[27] signifies having reached its end, finished, complete, perfect. Therefore, the revelation of God's law was complete before James wrote his epistle.

Luke (62 A.D.)

We have used the gospel according to Luke as a guideline in determining the dates of other books of the New Testament. We have done so with confidence that the evidence is strong enough to support this use. The most logical date for the writing of Luke's gospel is 62 A.D. while Luke was with Paul in Rome. There are several considerations which support this conclusion. (1) The author of the book also wrote the book of Acts, as indicated in the introduction of each book (Lk.1:3; Acts 1:1). (2) The book addresses the same person, Theophilus *(Ibid).* (3) In the book of Acts, the author interjects himself into the history of the book by his use of the plural pronouns *"we"* and *"us"* (cf.Acts 16:10,11; 20:5,6; 27:1; 28:16). Of all the traveling companions of Paul mentioned by name, and known to have been with him in Rome, all can be eliminated except Luke and Demas. (4) Luke was a physician (Col.4:14), and the author of Luke and Acts was exceptionally familiar with the use of medical terms and used them most frequently in these two New Testament books.[28] (5) The gospel of Luke was written prior to the book of Acts (Acts 1:1) which closes at the end of Paul's two years in Rome in 63 A.D. (Acts 28:30). So, the gospel of Luke was written sometime after Luke joined Paul at Philippi in 58 A.D. (Acts 20:5) and prior to 63 A.D. when the book of Acts ends.

Other considerations lend assistance in forming an opinion regarding the time and place of Luke's writing. (1) Theophilus is addressed as *"most excellent Theophilus"* (Lk.1:3). This title appears in Scripture only to address high ranking Roman officials (Acts 23:26; 24:3; 26:25). Accordingly, Theophilus appears to have been an official in the Roman government. There can be no question but that Paul's efforts in Rome reached into Nero's Palace (Phil.1:13) and at least some of *"Caesar's household"* were converted (Phil.4:22). Certainly, a Roman official would have been a part of Caesar's household. (2) It is interesting to note that conversions within Caesar's household were mentioned only to the Philippians, the place where the writer of the book of Acts spent seven years between 51 and 58 A.D. (Acts 16:16; 20:5). This evidence, at least, provides a reasonable explanation of the identity of Theophilus and the time of the writing of the Gospel of Luke. Accounting for the time necessary for the gospel to reach Caesar's household and conversions to take place, we would place the writing of this book in the summer or fall of 62 A.D.

Luke's gospel was written *"having followed all things closely for some time past,"* in order that Theophilus might have *"certainty concerning the things"* in which he had been instructed (Lk.1:3,4). Luke's statement testifies to the accuracy and reliability of the things revealed.[29] The only way Luke could have known the accuracy and reliability of the things he wrote, since he was not an eyewitness, was by inspiration of the Holy Spirit (1 Jn.2:20; 2 Tim.3:16,17). Furthermore, Luke wrote nothing new in this book. He said that his book was *"a narrative of the things that have been accomplished among us, just as those who from the beginning were eyewitnesses and ministers of the word have delivered them to us"* (Lk.1:1,2).

Notes

Lesson Exercises

Questions

1. List the six books Paul wrote between 52–58 A.D.:

2. Who quoted from Matthew's gospel and called it scripture?

3. Why do we place at least two gospel accounts before Luke?

4. Where was John Mark's hometown?

5. What did John Mark do that displeased Paul?

6. Identify the three men named James in the New Testament:

7. Why is it unreasonable to consider James, the brother of John, the author of James?

8. To whom does James address his book?

9. What pronouns in the book of Acts help to indicate the author of the book?

10. How long was Paul a prisoner in Rome?

Match

1. Matthew
2. Publican
3. Scripture
4. Nephew of Barnabas
5. The Lord's brother
6. Ananus
7. Law giver
8. Perfect
9. Luke
10. Nero's Palace

_____ Tax collector
_____ James
_____ One
_____ Caesar's household
_____ Philippi
_____ Levi
_____ Complete
_____ Inspired of God
_____ High Priest
_____ John Mark

True or False

1. _____ Dating the four gospels (Matthew, Mark, Luke, and John) is an easy task.

2. _____ Early tradition attributes the gospel of Matthew to the apostle by that name.

3. _____ Matthew does not harmonize with the other gospels.

4. _____ Luke was the first gospel account written.

5. _____ James, the brother of John, wrote the book of James.

6. _____ James, the brother of John, was killed in 44 A.D. by Herod Agrippa I.

7. _____ All truth was not completely revealed when James was written.

8. _____ The coming of the Lord was near when James was written (cf.Jas.5:7-9).

9. _____ Luke was with Paul while he was a prisoner in Rome.

10. _____ Luke had total confidence that what he had written was accurate.

Multiple Choice

1. The four gospels are **(prophetic, biographical, poetic)** in nature.

2. **(Matthew, Mark, Luke)** is thought to be the first of the four gospels written.

3. **(Matthew, Mark, John)** hosted a meal for Jesus (cf.Lk.5:29-32).

4. John Mark was with Paul on his **(first, second, third)** missionary journey.

5. Mark was with Peter in **(Rome, Babylon, Jerusalem)**.

6. The young man portrayed in Mark 14:51,52 is thought to be **(Matthew, Mark, Luke)**.

7. **(Mark, Luke, John)** was the disciple that Jesus loved.

8. The author of the gospel called "Luke" also wrote **(Acts, Romans, Revelation)**.

9. The books of Luke and Acts are addressed to **(Archippus, Silvanus, Theophilus)**.

10. The title "Most Excellent" would indicate that Theophilus was a **(Roman, Greek, Jewish)** official.

LESSON 08

PAUL'S PRISON EPISTLES

Paul's pen was silent for four years. He wrote the Romans in early 58 A.D. but did not write again until his first year of imprisonment in Rome. There he wrote Philippians, Ephesians, Colossians and Philemon.

Philippians (62 A.D.)

The first of Paul's prison epistles was Philippians. In this epistle, he expressed hope of being set free (cf.Phil.1:23-25; 2:24). He waited to *"see how it will go with me"* (Phil.2:23), indicating some degree of uncertainty. In the other epistles written from Rome, there was something more definite to report (cf.Eph.6:21,22; Col.4:7-9). To Philemon, he suggested the certainty of a visit (Phile.22). These things indicate that Philippians was written a little earlier than the other books, perhaps late in 62, or early in 63 A.D.

Paul had been in Rome for a good while when he wrote to the Philippians. The influence of the gospel preached by Paul in Rome, despite his bonds, had reached into all places, including the Palace (Phil.1:13). Weak-kneed preachers gained confidence after seeing Paul's boldness and were *"much more bold to speak the word without fear"* (Phil.1:14). Conflicts with false brethren developed (Phil.1:15-17). Word of Paul's imprisonment reached Philippi and a contribution was sent to relieve his needs (Phil.1:5-7; 2:25,26; 4:18). Epaphroditus, the messenger of the church in Philippi (Phil.2:25), overcame a sickness that nearly killed him (Phil.2:27) and was returning home (Phil.2:18). These things strongly imply Paul was in Rome well over a year before he wrote this epistle.

Philippians, like all the other New Testament books written to this point in time, contained only the doctrines previously revealed to its recipients. Paul said to them, *"To write the same things to you is no trouble to me and is safe for you"* (Phil.3:1). Again, *"Whereto we have already attained, let us walk by the same rule, let us mind the same thing... (Many walk, of whom I have told you often, and now tell you even weeping, that they are the enemies of the cross of Christ...)"* (Phil.3:16-19 KJV). These verses indicate that the rule by which the Philippians were to walk had already been revealed, and that this epistle contained *the same things* as those to which they had attained. There were no new revelations for the Philippians.

Ephesians (63 A.D.)

The second epistle written by Paul from Rome was the book of Ephesians. The epistle to the Colossians and the one to Philemon were also written in the same time period and delivered by the same messenger, Tychicus (cf.Eph.6:21; Col.4:7). As already indicated, the epistles to the Ephesians, Colossians, and to Philemon were written when Paul was fully convinced that he would be released from his bonds. They should be dated in the spring of 63 A.D.

There are some things in these epistles which raise questions regarding those addressed by Paul in the book of Ephesians. Is he actually addressing the church in Ephesus with which he had labored night and day for three years (cf.Acts 20:31)? Paul's statement, *"Because I have heard of your faith in the Lord Jesus and your love toward all the saints"* (Eph.1:15), does not indicate the close relationship with the Ephesians one would expect after three years among them. In fact, it strongly implies Paul had not met those addressed but had only heard of their faith. Again, he said, *"For this cause I Paul, the prisoner of Jesus Christ for you Gentiles, If ye have heard of the dispensation of the grace of God which is given me to you-ward"* (Eph.3:1,2 KJV). There could be no *"ifs"* about it. The Ephesians knew of Paul's ministry (cf.Acts 20:20,27,35). Those addressed in this epistle, however, were Gentiles who might not have heard of Paul's ministry to the Gentiles. Add to this the fact that Paul makes no mention of the Ephesians who were special to him as is characteristic of his epistles to churches where he was acquainted (cf.Rom.16:3; 1 Cor.16:19). This lack of personal interest strongly suggests the Ephesian epistle was not addressed to the Ephesian church Paul knew.

This problem is not a new discovery. The answer is probably found in the epistle to the Colossians. *"Give my greetings to the brothers at Laodicea, ... And when this letter has been read among you, have it also read in the church of the Laodiceans; and see that you also read the letter from Laodicea"* (Col.4:15,16). An epistle had been written to the Laodiceans apparently about the same time as the one written to the Colossians. Paul did not know either the Colossians or Laodiceans (cf.Col.2:1), which would explain his lack of personal interest being expressed in the Ephesian letter. In addition, the contents of the epistles to the Colossians and Ephesians are very similar in teaching and personal acquaintances. These facts lead many present-day students to conclude that this book was not addressed personally to the Ephesians but to the Laodiceans, or was a general circular epistle.[30]

Regardless of the answer to the problem, the epistle is authoritative containing the written revelation of the mystery which Paul preached. He said, *"How the mystery was made known to me by revelation, as I have written briefly. When you read this, you can perceive my insight into the mystery of Christ"* (Eph.3:3,4). Therefore, Paul affirms that the content of this epistle is the expression of his knowledge in the mystery which he had received by revelation of the Spirit. It is now preserved in writing so that we can read and understand it.

Colossians and Philemon (63 A.D.)

The books of Colossians and Philemon were written at the same time as the book of Ephesians. This places the date of these books also in the spring of 63 A.D., perhaps a few days or weeks before Paul was officially released from prison. His plea to Philemon, who was a resident of Colosse and a member of the church there (cf.Col.4:9; Phile.2,10,16), included a promise of a visit and a request for lodging (Phile.22). These considerations also indicate a date near the end of Paul's two-year Roman imprisonment (Acts 28:30).

Again, in this epistle Paul established the means of the production, reproduction and preservation of our New Testament Scriptures. Paul wrote, *"When this epistle is read among you, cause that it be read also in the church of the Laodiceans; and that ye likewise read the epistle from Laodicea"* (Col.4:16 KJV). The Thessalonians were to see that *"all of the holy brethren"* read their epistle, and the Colossians and Laodiceans were instructed to exchange epistles. Shortly, we will observe that this practice was widespread by 65 A.D.

Acts (63 A.D.)

It is apparent that the writing of the book of Acts follows the writing of the gospel of Luke (Acts 1:1). How long thereafter we do not know, but the abrupt end to the book of Acts indicates it was closed upon Paul's release from bondage and delivered before his party left Rome (Acts 28:30,31). Luke was with Paul in Rome at the time (cf. Col.4:14; Phile.24). He apparently stayed with Paul the remaining two or three years of his life as he journeyed through different parts of the world. He was with Paul when he returned to Rome the second time as prisoner (2 Tim.4:11). It appears highly unlikely that the book of Acts would have been completed after Paul's journey from Rome the first time without including further details of his activities. Therefore, we conclude that the book of Acts was completed by Luke in Rome and delivered to Theophilus sometime during the summer of 63 A.D.

The book of Acts proposes to be a continuation of the former treatise (Acts 1:1). It begins with the ascension of Christ, May 18, 30 A.D. and ends with Paul's release in Rome in 63 A.D. It contains the only running history we have of the beginning, early history, and growth of Christianity. Acts, therefore, serves an essential function without which our understanding of Christ and Christianity could not be complete. Surely, no one could believe for a moment that the book of Acts exists simply because Luke met Theophilus and desired to explain to him his faith. The vital link it provides between the life of Christ and the epistles written to the churches can only be explained from the standpoint of divine inspiration (2 Tim.3:16,17). The importance of this book to our New Testament canon should be apparent.

Hebrews (63 A.D.)

The book titled *"Hebrews"* is so called because it was directed toward those of the Israelite nation who were Christians. It was not intended originally to be directed toward every Christian Jew in the world, for the author informs them of his intended visit with them (Heb.13:23). With the Jews scattered throughout the world this would have been an impossibility. The substance of the book, particularly the discussion of the priesthoods, the importance of the temple of God to the fulfillment of the ordinances of divine service, the obvious references to Jerusalem as the place where these things were accomplished (cf.Heb.13:12,14), and the portrayal of the new heavenly Jerusalem which took the old city's place in the new order (Heb.12:22-24; cf.11:10,16), indicates that this epistle was directed to the church in Jerusalem and perhaps inclusive of the saints of Judea.

The author of the book is not named. For that reason, the book has been attributed to different ones, of whom the apostle Paul heads the list. The fact that Timothy is the author's traveling companion (Heb.13:23) and the letter is written from Italy (Heb.13:24) offers strong evidence for Paul's authorship.[31] We believe this to be the eleventh epistle penned by Paul.

The time of its writing would appear to be after Paul was released in Rome. He writes, *"You should know that our brother Timothy has been released, with whom I shall see you if he comes soon"* (Heb.13:23). There was no doubt about the author's ability to visit them. He indicated his freedom. When Paul wrote the Philippians, his first epistle penned in Rome, he proposed to send Timothy to them as soon as he saw how things would go (Phil.2:19-23). He also proposed that sometime thereafter he too would be able to come (Phil.2:24). When Paul wrote Philemon (Phile.22), he was convinced he would be released. We suggest that while Timothy was away on this mission, Paul wrote *"Hebrews."* When he said, *"Timothy has been released,"* he did not mean Timothy was released from prison but from the responsibilities placed upon him. Timothy fulfilled his mission and was returning to Paul.[32] During this interlude, Paul's release and Timothy's journey to Philippi, Paul probably visited the various churches in Italy (Heb.13:24) and wrote the letter to the Hebrews. We would date the epistle in the spring or summer of 63 A.D.

The book of Hebrews, like the rest, contains no doctrine that was new to these Jewish Christians. The author says that our great salvation *"was declared at first by the Lord, and it was attested to us by those who heard"* (Heb.2:3). If it was confirmed, there was nothing left to be confirmed. It was all revealed! Did Paul, then, write any new doctrine to them? Not at all! He referred to this epistle simply as *"my word of exhortation"* (Heb.13:22).

Notes

Lesson Exercises

True or False

1. _____ Paul had some expectation of being released from his imprisonment in Rome.
2. _____ The Philippians received no new revelations in the epistle written to them.
3. _____ Tychicus was the courier who delivered the books of Ephesians, Colossians and Philemon.
4. _____ Philemon was a member of the church in Ephesus.
5. _____ The book of Acts was written before the book of Luke.
6. _____ The book of Acts was written by Luke in Rome.
7. _____ The book of Acts contains our only running history of the early church.
8. _____ The book of Hebrews was written from Spain.

Questions

1. Name the four books Paul wrote during his first imprisonment in Rome:

2. Which one of these is thought to be the first to be written?

3. What church sent gifts to Paul on numerous occasions?

4. Why would anyone think the book of Ephesians is actually the Laodiceans?

5. What principle is established in Colossians 4:16?

6. At what point in time does the book of Acts end?

7. As best you can, explain why it is thought that the book of Hebrews is directed only at the Jews in Jerusalem and, perhaps, Judea:

Lesson 08 - Paul's Prison Epistles

Fill In The Blank

1. "Let us _____ by the _____ rule, let us _____ the _____ thing" (Phil.3:16 KJV).

2. Some authorities think the book of _____ is the book Paul wrote to the Laodicians (cf.Col.4:16).

3. "How the _____ was made _____ to me by _____, as I have written briefly. When you read this, you can _____ _____ _____ into the mystery of Christ" (Eph.3:3,4).

4. Paul made a request for _____ from Philemon when he came (Phile.22).

5. "And when this letter has been read among you, have it also _____ in the church of the _____; and see that you _____ read the letter from Laodicea" (Col.4:16).

6. "You should know that our brother _____ has been _____, with whom I shall _____ you if he comes soon" (Heb.13:23).

7. "It was declared at first by the _____, and it was _____ to us by those who _____" (Heb.2:3).

Match

1. Was from Colosse
2. Bonds
3. Messenger from Philippi
4. Delivered Colossians & Ephesians
5. Hebrews
6. Temple of God
7. Paul's traveling companion
8. 62 A.D.
9. 63 A.D.
10. 30 A.D.

____ Tychicus
____ Divine service
____ Philemon
____ Jesus' Ascension
____ Philippians written
____ Epaphroditus
____ Ephesians written
____ Timothy
____ Jewish Christians
____ Paul

LESSON 09

THE POST PRISON EPISTLES

The Prevailing Winds

During the years of Paul's imprisonment, the winds of revolt among the Jews of Judea began to blow strongly. The procurators sent by the Caesars were ruthless tyrants who raped and robbed the people.[33] Their miseries grew worse and worse until the Jews scattered throughout the world began to be involved in sharing those miseries.[34] Their frequent trips to Jerusalem for the feasts placed them in favorable position to carry the alarms of war into the distant communities of the Dispersion. It appears that as early as 64 A.D., Jewish teachers, under the guise of Christianity, were entering into Christian homes rallying support for the approaching conflict in Palestine (cf.Titus 1:10,11). Efforts on the part of the Jews were clothed in promises of liberty for Jews everywhere (cf.2 Pet.2; Jude). Such attempts by the Jews were practiced for a number of years according to Josephus.[35] Doubtless, as the flames of passion for war with the Romans rose, these filthy dreamers waded through the cities of the world rallying support for their cause. In the spring of 65 A.D., at the feast of unleavened bread, three million Jews laid their case against Procurator Florus before Cestius Gallus, President of Syria, who did nothing about their complaints. The passions of the pilgrims were aroused by his inaction. It is only reasonable to assume that these millions of pilgrims returned to their homes with renewed determination to rally support for the inevitable conflict. It is in the midst of these prevailing winds that the remainder of the New Testament books were written.

In the absence of a running historical record, such as the book of Acts, guidelines for dating are not as certain during the middle 60's as they were before. There are a few helpful things revealed. Luke's historical record ended in the spring of 63 A.D. The writing of Hebrews likely took place in the spring or summer of the same year. Paul indicated in Hebrews that he intended to visit Jerusalem (Heb.13:19,23). A direct course to Jerusalem from Rome was a long journey, approximately 1500 miles. Five to six months were required for Paul's journey to Rome in 60 A.D., though three months of that time were spent wintering on Melita (Acts 28:11). If Paul and his companions left Rome in the summer months of 63 A.D., they could have reached Jerusalem by early fall of the year. Even if they left Rome in the early fall, they could have reached Jerusalem before winter. We suggest the possibility of their leaving Rome, traveling as far as Crete, where Paul left Titus to *"put what remained into order"* (Titus 1:5), before moving on to other destinations. Whether he went on to Jerusalem or directly into Asia, where we have evidence of his presence in later epistles, we cannot determine. The time elements involved indicate that he was in Asia no later than the late spring of 64 A.D.

1 Peter (64 A.D.)

Prior to Paul's release from prison in Rome, John Mark came to Paul and was with him at the time he wrote to the Colossians (Col.4:10; Phile.24). Paul instructed the Colossians, *"if he comes to you, welcome him."* This indicated that Mark intended to travel through that region shortly. When the apostle Peter wrote his first epistle from Babylon, Mark was with him (1 Pet.5:13). The path from Rome to Babylon is a direct one, passing through the regions of *"Pontus, Galatia, Cappadocia, Asia, and Bithynia,"* the areas to which Peter addressed himself (1 Pet.1:1). We suggest the possibility of Mark passing through these regions as he traveled from Rome to Babylon. Learning from Mark the extensive trials the people of the region were suffering may well have prompted Peter to direct this first letter to them, comforting and encouraging them in their trials. These trials no doubt were the beginning of sorrows that were to be suffered throughout the whole world in the great tribulation period that was to precede the destruction of Jerusalem (cf.Lk.21:25-32,34-36; 1 Pet.4:1,7,12,17,18; Rev.3:10; 14:14-16). The tone of Paul's first letter to Timothy, which fits into this time period, strongly implies intense pressures from both Roman and Jewish loyalists (cf.1 Pet.1:6-11; 2:1-6; 6:12-16). We believe the most likely date for the writing of 1 Peter is the summer of 64 A.D. The epistle was delivered by Silvanus (Silas, 1 Pet.5:12), Paul's traveling companion on the *second* missionary journey.

This epistle, like the others, contains no new teaching. The people of the regions addressed had received the news of salvation *"through those who preached the good news to you by the Holy Spirit sent from heaven"* (1 Pet.1:12). *"This word is the good news that was preached to you"* and *"declaring that this is the true grace of God. Stand firm in it"* (1 Pet.1:25; 5:12). Long before Peter wrote this epistle, these Christians were standing in the full grace of God.

Titus (64 A.D.)

In the meantime, as Peter, from Babylon, was writing to the saints scattered throughout the northern regions of Asia Minor, Paul journeyed toward Asia. He desired to visit Colosse (Phile.24) and he passed through Ephesus where he left Timothy to *"charge certain persons not to teach any different doctrine"* (1 Tim.1:3). From Ephesus he went into Macedonia. This visit to Asia and Macedonia likely took place in the spring and summer of 64 A.D.

Sometime during this period, Paul, apparently in Macedonia, wrote Titus, whom he had left on Crete. He proposed that shortly he would send Artemas or Tychicus, at which time he desired Titus to come to him at Nicopolis, probably in Achaia, where he planned to spend the winter (Titus 3:12). Paul expected that there would be time for Titus to complete the work assigned before coming to Nicopolis. If Paul spent the winter of 64 and 65 A.D. in Nicopolis, he was possibly in Macedonia when Rome burned, July 19, 64 A.D. This would place Paul in those regions during the first Roman persecution of Christians, which took place in mid-November of the same year.[36]

Paul's instructions to Titus were designed to encourage him to complete the work he was left on Crete to do. Even the Cretians were fully taught of God, for Titus was instructed to *"put them in mind,"* or *"remind them"*[37] of their responsibilities (Titus 3:1). There is no evidence of new revelation in Titus.

1 Timothy (64 A.D.)

Paul wrote to Timothy not long after leaving him at Ephesus. Yet, it appears that he wrote to him *after* leaving Macedonia (1 Tim.1:3). If this is the case, Paul apparently wrote the first epistle to Timothy from Achaia, perhaps from Nicopolis, where he had planned to winter. We would place the time of the writing as late in 64 A.D., or very early in 65 A.D. Paul wrote the epistle with the expectation of returning to Ephesus where he had left Timothy (1 Tim.3:14; 4:13). From all indications, Paul fulfilled his wishes, though it may have been an unhappy return (cf.2 Tim.1:4; 4:13-15).

Timothy was fully equipped to teach the truth in its fullness. He knew the doctrine so that he could continue in it (1 Tim.4:16) and was inspired with a spiritual gift so that he had access to the revelation of truth (1 Tim.4:14; 2 Tim.1:6). The saints at Ephesus were likewise informed of the truth for Timothy was to *"put these things before the brothers"* (1 Tim.4:6). So, this epistle, like the others, contains no new doctrines.

2 Peter (65 A.D.)

Paul visited with the Ephesian elders at Miletus in the spring of 58 A.D. He said to them, *"I know that after my departure fierce wolves will come in among you, not sparing the flock; and from among your own selves will arise men speaking twisted things, to draw away the disciples after them"* (Acts 20:29,30). Six years later when Paul returned to Ephesus, he found that his prophecy had been fulfilled. Some were teaching other doctrines (1 Tim.1:3). Some were *"desiring to be teachers of the law"* (1 Tim.1:7). Five different men, Hymenaeus, Alexander, Phygelus, Hermogenes and Philetus (1 Tim.1:20; 2 Tim.1:15; 2:17), were named as apostates and labeled as teaching doctrines contrary to the truth. The implications are that many other false teachers had invaded the area, and Timothy was warned to be on the guard against them (1 Tim.1:19,20; 4:1-3; 6:3-5,20,21; 2 Tim.1:15; 2:14-18,23-26; 3:1-13; 4:1-4,14,15). During the six years of Paul's absence from Asia, a general state of decay set in, threatening to destroy the church throughout all of Asia Minor.

This state of affairs was expected. Jesus foretold that these conditions would develop prior to the final destruction of Jerusalem. He said, *"Then they will deliver you up to tribulation and put you to death, and you will be hated by all nations for my name's sake. And then many will fall away and betray one another and hate one another. And many false prophets will arise and lead many astray. And because lawlessness will be increased, the love of many will grow cold. But the one who endures to the end will be saved. And this gospel of the kingdom will be proclaimed throughout the whole world as a testimony to all nations, and then the end will come"* (Matt.24:9-14). These conditions developed as Jesus foretold, not only in Asia Minor, but throughout the world. James reminded the Jewish brethren of these approaching events (Jas.5:7-11), and Peter directed his first epistle to the Christians of Asia Minor to remind them these things were at hand (1 Pet.4:7-19). Paul's warning, then, to the Ephesian elders (Acts 20:29,30) and to Timothy, was the signal that *"the last days"* of the Jewish economy were upon them (cf.1 Tim.4:1; 2 Tim.3:1).

This is the prevailing atmosphere surrounding the writing of the rest of the New Testament books. The second epistle of Peter fits into the mood of the hour. Perhaps, when Silvanus delivered the *first* epistle of Peter, he saw what Paul had seen in Asia and returned to Babylon with the news of the developing situation. This may have prompted Peter to write this *second* epistle (cf.2 Pet.3:1). Peter's purpose is apparent. He sought to establish the unchangeable nature of revealed truth (2 Pet.1:3,13-21; 3:1-7), and to warn against the false teachers arising in the church (2 Pet.2:1-22). These false teachers may have been rallying support for the approaching Judean conflict. This epistle was probably written within a year of the first epistle of Peter and should be dated around the summer of 65 A.D.

In this epistle Peter seeks to establish the completeness of divine revelation and the place of the epistles in God's scheme for preserving His revelation for all times. He said, *"His divine power has granted to us all things that pertain to life and godliness, through the knowledge of him who called us to his own glory and excellence"* (2 Pet.1:3). In other words, Peter affirmed that we have everything we need for *"life and godliness."* He then argues for the purpose of the epistles. *"Therefore I intend always to remind you of these qualities, though you know them and are established in the truth that you have. I think it right, as long as I am in this body, to stir you up by way of reminder"* (2 Pet.1:12,13). Again, *"This is now the second letter that I am writing to you, beloved. In both of them I am stirring up your sincere mind by way of reminder, that you should remember the predictions of the holy prophets and the commandment of the Lord and Savior through your apostles"* (2 Pet.3:1,2). These epistles were simply reminders of the truth which they already knew and contained no new teaching whatsoever.

In closing his second epistle, Peter confirmed the principle that Paul instituted for the development, production, reproduction and preservation of the written New Testament (cf.1 Thess.5:27; Col.4:16). He said, *"And count the patience of our Lord as salvation, just as our beloved brother Paul also wrote to you according to the wisdom given him, as he does in all his letters when he speaks in them of these matters. There are some things in them that are hard to understand, which the ignorant and unstable twist to their own destruction, as they do the other Scriptures"* (2 Pet.3:15,16). This statement established (1) the acceptability of Paul and his writings. (2) It established the workability of Paul's plan for reproducing his epistles, since Peter had read most of them. (3) It recognized the classification of Paul's epistles as *"scripture"* thus establishing their inspiration (2 Tim.3:15-17; 2 Pet.1:20,21). This is a marvelous thing because this statement provides inspired testimony to the actual process of the development of our New Testament scriptures.

Lesson Exercises

Questions

1. Who is thought to be the author of Hebrews?

2 Approximately how far from Jerusalem was Rome?

3. How long did it take Paul to journey from Caesarea to Rome?

4. How much of that time was spent on Melita?

5. Which former companion of Paul was with him when he wrote Colossians?

6. Whom did Paul instruct to receive Marcus when he came?

7. To whom does Peter address his first epistle?

8. When Paul left Timothy at Ephesus, where did he go?

9. Where was Titus when Paul wrote to him?

10. Did Paul expect to see Timothy again when he wrote 1 Timothy?

11. How did Timothy receive his spiritual gift?

12. What warning did Paul give the Ephesian elders (Acts 20:29,30)?

13. Did Paul's warning come true?

14. Did Jesus foretell an era when false teachers would arise?

True and False

1. _____ Silas was Paul's traveling companion on his 2nd missionary journey.

2. _____ Hermogenes was a faithful gospel preacher.

3. _____ The "last days" always identify the Christian age.

4. _____ The Epistles contained new teaching.

5. _____ Paul at times wrote things difficult to understand.

Fill In The Blank

1. The Christians Peter addressed received the news of salvation "through _____ who preached the _____ _____ to you" (1 Pet.1:12).

2. "This _____ is the good news that was _____ to you" (1 Pet.1:25).

3. Peter wrote "exhorting and declaring that _____ ____ the true grace of God. Stand _____ in it" (1 Pet.5:12).

4. Timothy was to "charge certain persons not to teach ____ _____ _____" (1 Tim.1:3).

5. Titus was told to "_____ them" (Titus 3:1).

6. To the Ephesians Timothy was to "put these things _____ the brothers." (1 Tim.4:6).

7. "His divine power _____ _____ to us _____ _____ that pertain to _____ and _____" (2 Pet.1:3).

8. "Therefore I intend always to _____ you of these qualities, though you _____ them and are established in the _____ that you have" (2 Pet.1:12).

9. "This is now the second letter that I am writing to you, beloved. In _____ of them I am stirring up your sincere mind by way of _____" (2 Pet.3:1).

Match

1. Josephus
2. Florus
3. Cestius Gallus
4. Titus
5. Miletus
6. Philetus
7. Silas
8. Artemas
9. Nicopolis
10. Burning of Rome
11. Destruction of Jerusalem
12. Paul's epistles

_____ President of Syria
_____ Scripture
_____ Ephesian Elders
_____ Paul wintered there
_____ Jewish Historian
_____ Tychicus
_____ False teacher
_____ 70 A.D.
_____ Procurator of Judea
_____ Left on Crete
_____ 64 A.D.
_____ Silvanus

LESSON 10

THE POST PRISON EPISTLES CONTINUED

Jude (65 A.D.)

In our previous lesson, we learned of departures from the truth and the false teachers invading the churches. The Apostles, Peter and Paul, addressed these problems in their epistles written during this time. News of these apostasies reached Jerusalem. James had been in the forefront of leadership in dealing with such problems, but he was now dead. It appears that his brother Jude (Jude 1) arose to meet the demands of the hour. Perhaps, from the standpoint of teaching, it was not necessary that another voice be heard because the saints by this time were amply warned. To hear a voice from Jerusalem, the city soon to be destroyed, would have had a strengthening and stabilizing effect upon the faithful throughout the world.

The similarity of language and argumentation to 2 Peter 2 places the epistle of Jude in the same time period as 2 Peter. We shall see shortly that this also places them in the same time period as the epistles of John and the Revelation. Due to the mood of the Jerusalem Jews at that time, we would date the writing of Jude's epistle in the summer of 65 A.D.

There can be no doubt about Jude's intention in the epistle. He wrote to urge the saints *"to contend for the faith that was once for all delivered to the saints"* (Jude 3). The faith had long before been revealed, even before any of it was penned. But false teachers had crept in, as God had forewarned (Jude 4,17,18). Jude wrote to call those saints into remembrance of those warnings concerning the days that were coming (Jude 5,17). There are no new doctrines taught in this epistle.

2 Timothy (65 A.D.)

In our last reference to Paul's whereabouts in this time period, we reflected upon his plans to winter in Nicopolis, Achaia where he likely wrote 1 Timothy. In this epistle, he expressed plans of returning shortly to Ephesus (cf.1 Tim.3:14; 4:13). Later, Paul wrote 2 Timothy in which it is apparent that he was a prisoner again. He offered no explanation of his capture to Timothy which leads us to reason that Timothy already knew the details of Paul's circumstances. Furthermore, Paul makes no mention of his expected return to Ephesus which also implies that he did indeed return to Ephesus prior to writing this *second* epistle.

There are three things mentioned in Paul's second epistle to Timothy which strongly suggest that Paul did return to Ephesus, not as a free man but as a prisoner. (1) For some unexplained reason Paul left his cloak, books and parchments in Troas with Carpus (2 Tim.4:13). It does not seem likely that he would have left them there when going into Macedonia for he planned to winter before returning. Also, he wrote two epistles while in Macedonia and Achaia which indicates the presence of his parchments with him there. It is highly unlikely that he would have left these things at Troas while on an extended journey. The uncertainty of his fortunes would have prevented such presumption. This leads one to the possible conclusion that on his way back into Asia, Paul stopped briefly in Troas and while there ran into difficulties that resulted in his arrest. If so, Paul most likely was transported to Ephesus, the provincial capital, for trial where he again exercised his rights as a Roman citizen and, appealing to Caesar, was sent to Rome. The suddenness of such activity would have prevented him from picking up his belongings. (2) Paul mentions Timothy's tears in this epistle (2 Tim.1:4) which suggests a departure from Timothy that was much different than any before. Perhaps the reason is very understandable. The news of the terrible atrocities against the Roman Christians by Nero, late in 64 A.D., would have reached this region by the spring of 65 A.D. With Paul's capture and Rome as his destination, there can be no doubt about the thoughts that must have raced through Timothy's mind as he bade Paul farewell on this occasion. His tears would have flowed as rivers and apparently, they did. Why else would Paul make special mention of them in this epistle? (3) Paul passed through Miletus at some time in this period leaving Trophimus there sick (2 Tim.4:20). Miletus was approximately 35 miles from Ephesus indicating that Paul was in that region briefly before going to Rome as a prisoner. If these deductions are anywhere near correct, Paul's final arrest came in the late spring or early summer of 65 A.D.

Shortly after Paul arrived in Rome, he made his defense before the Roman court with no one to defend him (2 Tim.4:16). The difficulties in Rome had caused all to forsake him (2 Tim.4:10,16). Only Luke remained with him (2 Tim.4:11). Seeing his plight and knowing that his end was near (2 Tim.4:6), Paul wrote Timothy to come to him before winter and to bring Mark (2 Tim.4:9,11,21). Mark was with Peter in Babylon when 1 Peter was written in 64 A.D. (1 Pet.5:13), but at this time appears to be in the regions around Ephesus. Perhaps he had delivered Peter's second epistle to the churches and was in Ephesus having completed the delivery. We suggest that 2 Timothy was written in the late summer or early fall of 65 A.D.

Paul's purpose in writing this epistle to Timothy, apart from his desire for Timothy to come to him, was to strengthen, encourage and prepare Timothy for continued faithfulness during the stiff trials to come (2 Tim.1:6,7; 2:1-7,11-13,15-17,22-26; 3:14-17; 4:1-5). Paul knew these trials were coming. They had all been forewarned of them, and it was now time for Timothy to learn to stand on his own two feet and be courageous. Again, this epistle was not written to reveal new truth. Timothy already knew *"the pattern of the sound words"* (2 Tim.1:13), but now it was his responsibility to see that others were instructed fully so that they could continue to teach the gospel (2 Tim.2:2).

The Works of John

To this point, we have said practically nothing about the writings of the apostle John to whom five New Testament books are attributed. For the most part, Bible students have assigned the writings of these books to the last few years of the first century. This removes them by at least twenty-thirty years from the production period of the other New Testament books. There have been a number of reasons for this: (1) The works of John are not quoted by any of the early church writers until late in the second century. This is thought to indicate an authorship later than the other New Testament books. (2) The style of writing is thought to be identified with a period of time later than that of the other writers. (3) The pains John takes making sure his students understand the Jewish culture lead some to conclude John wrote when the culture had changed; a time period following the destruction of Jerusalem. (4) The portrayal of *"Emperor Worship"* in the book of Revelation leads many to think the book was written when the practice was at an advanced stage. These reasons have forced most Bible students to conclude that the books of John were written late in the first century, probably between 90 and 96 A.D.

The foregoing conclusions are not those of this writer. Does it stand to reason that twenty-thirty years should stand between John's writings and the rest of the New Testament? Since *"all truth"* had long before been revealed, *i.e.*, by 50 A.D. or shortly thereafter, what possible reason could there be for waiting this late to finish the writing of it? These and many other questions can be raised to which there are no valid answers. Yet, all the aforementioned reasons given to establish a late writing of John's works can be readily answered. The following comment concerning the Dead Sea Scrolls' relationship to the writings of John will demonstrate that early dates for John's works are tenable:

> "The Dead Sea Material has had a stabilizing effect upon New Testament criticism. In the light of the new material, the New Testament appears as a Jewish book with a Christian theology with less Greek influence in its formation than Jewish, and there is reason to date the synoptic gospels beginning with Mark between A.D. 60 and 65.
>
> "Especially interesting is the date of the Gospel of John. A radical criticism customarily dated this Gospel about A.D. 150 or later. Thus, it was effectually removed from apostolic tradition and treated more as an apocryphal book. Now it is well known that the Fourth Gospel reflects the genuine Jewish background of John the Baptist and Jesus and not a later second-century Gnostic milieu. This is clearly attested by the parallels to the conceptual imagery of John's Gospel in the Essenic Literature from Qumran.
>
> "There is every evidence to believe in the authenticity of John's Gospel, and there is not the slightest reason critically to date the Gospel after A.D. 90. Indeed, it may be quite a bit earlier. Thus, the Dead Sea discoveries and the excavations at Qumran not only give additional background material to the inter-biblical and New Testament period, but also help to stabilize higher criticism and purge out radical views that are now shown not to be tenable.
>
> "Also, the Book of Revelation was doubtless penned toward the end of the first century, and, in light of the Dead Sea Scrolls may now possibly be dated earlier, i.e., before A.D. 70. This conclusion is based on its Hebraic background, being illuminated by the evidence from the Dead Sea manuscripts."[38]

This quotation is lengthy but useful in demonstrating that the arguments used to prove a late date for John's writings are not conclusive. We believe, however, there are conclusive proofs which assign these books to the same time period as the other New Testament books, and we shall present this proof in due time.

Lesson Exercises

Questions

1. The book of Jude is similar in language to what other N.T. book?

2. What other books fit into the same time frame as Jude?

3. Why did Jude write?

4. What three things in 2 Timothy indicate that Paul returned to Ephesus?

5. Who defended Paul during his first defense before Caesar's court in Rome?

6. Whom did Paul instruct Timothy to bring with him to Rome?

7. Why did Paul write 2 Timothy?

8. How many N.T. books are attributed to John? Name them:

9. In your opinion, does it stand to reason that we should separate John's writings by 25 years from the other N.T. books? If yes, explain?

10. What recent discovery has had a stabilizing effect upon N.T. criticism?

True or False

1. _____ Paul wrote two epistles while in Macedonia and Achaia on his last trip there.

2. _____ Timothy's tears were caused from being homesick.

3. _____ Domitian instigated a persecution against Christians in Rome in 64 A.D.

4. _____ Miletus was about 35 miles from Rome.

5. _____ Nero blamed the burning of Rome on Christians.

6. _____ Nero fiddled while Rome burned.

7. _____ Many believe Nero was the one responsible for the burning of Rome.

8. _____ Paul revealed new truth to Timothy in his second epistle to him.

9. _____ The works of John are not quoted until late in the second century.

10. _____ The Dead Sea Scrolls have opened the door for a consideration of the works of John being written before 70 A.D.

Multiple Choice

1. Jude wrote to urge saints to **(deny, accept, contend for)** the faith.

2. In 1 Timothy, Paul expressed plans to return shortly to **(Corinth, Antioch, Ephesus)**.

3. When Paul wrote 2 Timothy, he was in **(Caesarea, Rome, Philippi)** as a prisoner.

4. **(Luke, Demas, Timothy)** was the only companion of Paul to remain with him in Rome during this second imprisonment.

5. Paul wanted Timothy to come to him before **(summer, fall, winter)**.

6. The works of John are usually assigned to the years of **(60–66; 70–78, 90–96)** A.D.

7. The Dead Sea Scrolls were discovered in the **(18th, 19th, 20th)** century.

8. "All Truth" was revealed by **(50, 60, 70)** A.D.

Lesson 10 - The Post Prison Epistles

Match

1. Brother of Jude
2. Books
3. Carpus
4. The Capital of Asia
5. Roman citizen
6. Tears
7. Trophimus
8. Peter
9. Revelation
10. Dead Sea Scrolls

_____ Ephesus
_____ James
_____ Paul
_____ Babylon
_____ Sick
_____ Emperor worship
_____ Parchments
_____ Qumran
_____ Timothy
_____ Troas

Notes

LESSON 11

THE WORKS OF JOHN

The Man John

We need to say something about John, the elusive man to whom five books of our New Testament are attributed. He was the brother of James, the first apostle to die a martyr (Acts 12:1,2). He, Peter and James constituted what is often called the *"inner circle"* of Christ's disciples (Matt.17:1; 26:37). He referred to himself as *"the disciple whom Jesus loved"* (Jn.21:20,24; 13:23). He and Peter worked together in Jerusalem following Pentecost and bore the brunt of the early persecutions (Acts 3:1; 4:3,13). He, Peter and James, the Lord's brother, were *"pillars"* in the church at Jerusalem when Paul was there for the conference in 49 or 50 A.D. (Gal.2:9). After this, however, John was not mentioned by name again until he penned the Apocalypse.

Where was John during these years? Why do we not have any inspired information about him? Some have reasoned that, since Jesus entrusted the care of His mother to John (Jn.19:26,27), he stayed in Jerusalem caring for Mary until she died and then went into Asia Minor. This conclusion is without foundation.

As the Jerusalem Conference was breaking up, James, Cephas and John extended the right hands of fellowship to Paul and Barnabas to go unto the heathen *"and they to the circumcised"* (Gal.2:9). James stayed in Jerusalem (Acts 21:18). Peter was later seen in Antioch (Gal.2:11), then in Babylon (1 Pet.5:13). We suggest that Peter passed through Antioch on his way to Babylon, the area he chose for his activity. There were large numbers of Jews living in Babylon.[39] This was the logical place for Peter to go. Where did John go? Galatians 2:9 indicates that he was going somewhere. Our only clue is in the Apocalypse (Rev.1:9) where he identified Patmos, off the coast of Asia, as the place of residence at that time. Could he have spent these years in Asia Minor?

When Paul and Silas passed through Asia Minor on the second missionary journey in 50-51 A.D., they were forbidden to preach the gospel in Asia, Bithynia or Mysia (Acts 16:6-8). To our knowledge, Paul preached only in the cities of Ephesus and Troas in these regions, and that was on his third missionary journey. We learn, however, that there were churches in Asia in 57 A.D. (1 Cor.16:19), and in 63 A.D. there were churches in Laodicea, Hierapolis and Colosse, none of which were known personally to Paul (Col.2:1; 4:13). Then we learn from Peter that in 64 A.D. there were churches scattered throughout Pontus, Galatia, Cappadocia, Asia and Bithynia (1 Pet.1:1). These brethren heard the gospel preached by inspired men (1 Pet.1:12) and received spiritual gifts by the laying on of an apostle's hands (1 Pet.4:10; cf.Acts 8:17-19). Which apostle performed this service? Paul had certainly done so in Galatia and in parts of Asia, but not in Pontus, Cappadocia or Bithynia. Could it have been Peter, since he addressed himself to them? It was not Peter for it is clear that Peter was not personally acquainted with these brethren (cf.1 Pet.1:12). If Peter intended to identify the apostle who went among the people of this region as an eyewitness of the transfiguration by his statement in 2 Peter 1:16-18, then that apostle was John. Only Peter, James and John were eyewitnesses of His transfiguration. James at this time had been dead for twenty years, and Peter apparently did not personally know the ones addressed. While this argument does not fully satisfy the need for an explanation, it does pose some interesting considerations. Why, of all the events involving the apostles that give evidence of the divinity of Jesus, did Peter select the transfiguration to make his point? If John was the apostle who preached to them, the question has a simple answer. We suggest the possibility of John's working through the northern sections of Asia Minor, going westward until the whole of Asia Minor was completely evangelized.

The Gospel of John (60-64 A.D.?)

We previously suggested the possibility that the Gospel of John was written prior to the writing of Luke. It could be one of the accounts of the life of Christ referred to as written before the Gospel of Luke (Lk.1:1). This would have demanded a date earlier than 62 A.D. This is not unreasonable. One thing is sure, it was written before 70 A.D. and before the death of Peter. John wrote, *"Now there is in Jerusalem by the Sheep Gate a pool, in Aramaic called Bethesda, which has five roofed colonnades"* (Jn.5:2). Note the present tense: "there is." If John wrote after 70 A.D. that statement should read *"there was!"* Jerusalem was destroyed in 70 A.D. If the Gospel was written after 70 A.D., John was ignorant of Jerusalem's destruction. Even more unbelievable is the fact that the Holy Spirit directed the mistake. Who can believe it? He who does must rely upon the testimony of two witnesses who reported a thing as existing that did not exist! This position undermines the reliability of every other piece of information recorded in the book. However, if we implicitly trust John and the Holy Spirit, the conclusion *must be* that Jerusalem was still standing when John penned this Gospel.

Furthermore, after Jesus had explained to Peter how it would be in his old age, John adds, *"This he said to show by what kind of death he was to glorify God"* (Jn.21:19). The phrase "he was to glorify God" was softened by the translators to make it appear the author wrote the phrase after the death of Peter. We can understand how translators could do this if they believed in the late authorship, but the expression literally forecast a future event at the time of writing. Literally, John said, *"And this he said signifying by what death he will glorify God."*[40] This places the death of Peter as still in the future when this Gospel was written. Later, when Peter penned his second epistle, he made reference to his impending death indicating that the people addressed already knew the details of how that death would take place (2 Pet.1:14). The Gospel of John was written before 70 A.D., possibly in 60 or 61 A.D., but not later than 64 A.D., because it must pre-date the first epistle of John (cf.1 Jn.1:1-5).

The Gospel of John was written in order that we *"may believe that Jesus is the Christ, the Son of God, and that by believing you may have life in his name"* (Jn.20:31). John testified of these things in his preaching. He then wrote them down in order that the effect of his gospel might continue (Jn.21:24).

John's Gospel gives us the fourth separate record of the life of Christ we have to draw on. The variations in these accounts have led many critics to attack the Bible and Christianity as being built upon an unstable foundation. John's Gospel in particular has been attacked for containing contradictions, which supposedly undermine the trustworthiness of the accounts. The facts, however, are to the contrary. John's Gospel solves the supposed difficulties. The Holy Spirit, knowing that in time much of the Jewish culture would be lost and our understanding impaired, anticipated the problem and corrected it in the Gospel of John. When John's explanations are understood in the light of Jewish culture and the teaching of the law of Moses, every supposed difficulty disappears. This Gospel is a most important production.

The Epistles of John (64 or 65 A.D.)

The epistles of John must be identified with the same time period as 2 Peter, Jude and 2 Timothy. All four authors identify false teachers with similar characteristics cast into a time period known as *"the last days"* (2 Tim.3:1; 2 Pet.3:3; Jude 17,18; 1 Jn.2:18). These *"last days"* identify the last days of the Jewish nation. The false teachers are referred to as *"men corrupted in mind and disqualified regarding the faith"* (2 Tim.3:8), *"false prophets"* (2 Pet.2:1), *"ungodly people"* (Jude 4) and *"antichrist"* (1 Jn.2:18). They had been a part of the church (2 Tim.3:5; 2 Pet.2:1; Jude 4; 1 Jn.2:22,23; 4:3), were without the Spirit of God (2 Tim.3:5; 2 Pet.2:17; Jude 19; 1 Jn.4:1,6), were deceivers (2 Tim.3:13; 2 Pet.2:13; Jude 16,18; 2 Jn.7), and fulfilled the lusts of the flesh (2 Tim.3:2,4,6; 2 Pet.2:10,18; 3:3; Jude 4,8,16,18; 1 Jn.2:15,16; 4:5).

More could be said to show that all four authors identify the same false teachers and the same time period. In speaking of the spirit of antichrist John said, *"You heard was coming and now is in the world already"* (1 Jn.4:3). This was at the beginning of the period. Jude said, *"You must remember, beloved, the predictions of the apostles of our Lord Jesus Christ. They said to you, "In the last time there will be scoffers, following their own ungodly passions." It is these who cause divisions, worldly people, devoid of the Spirit"* (Jude 17-19). Paul and Peter's message were the same (cf.2 Tim.3:1-5; 2 Pet.3:1-3). John said, *"It is the last hour, and as you have heard that antichrist is coming, so now many antichrists have come"* (1 Jn.2:18). Since the time period for all these epistles is the same, we would place the writing of John's epistles in late 64, or early 65 A.D.

It is evident that John's epistles fit the same pattern as the other New Testament books. They contain no new doctrines. He said, *"But you have been anointed by the Holy One, and you all have knowledge. I write to you, not because you do not know the truth, but because you know it, and because no lie is of the truth... you have no need that anyone should teach you. But as his anointing teaches you about everything, and is true, and is no lie—just as it has taught you, abide in him"* (1 Jn.2:20,21,27; cf.2 Jn.5,9-11; 3 Jn.3).

Notes

Lesson Exercises

True or False

1. _____ Peter was the disciple that Jesus loved.
2. _____ Peter preached many times in Pontus, Galatia, Cappadocia, and Bithynia.
3. _____ We know for certain the Gospel of John was written around 90–96 A.D.
4. _____ John 5:2 shows Jerusalem still stood when John wrote his gospel.
5. _____ John 21:19 indicates that Peter was dead when John's gospel was written.
6. _____ John's gospel contradicts the other three gospels.
7. _____ The gospel of John is a very important production.
8. _____ The Antichrists were not Christians.
9. _____ We are to look for the Antichrist who will appear on the scene any day now.
10. _____ The epistles of John reveal new truth.

Questions

1. What three apostles constituted the "inner circle" of Jesus' disciples?

2. Which apostles were considered "pillars" in the church at Jerusalem?

3. What two apostles bore the brunt of the early persecutions against the saints?

4. Which apostle was given the responsibility of caring for Jesus' mother?

5. After the Jerusalem conference, who went to preach to the gentiles?

6. Where was Paul forbidden to preach?

7. What two places outside Jerusalem was Peter seen following the Conference?

8. What event in the life of Christ links John to preaching in Asia Minor?

9. What is the stated purpose of the gospel of John?

10. In your opinion, what is the meaning of the expression "the last time"?

Lesson 11 - The Works of John

Fill In The Blank

1. The cities of Asia where we know Paul preached were _____ & _____.

2. "Now _____ _____ in Jerusalem by the _____ _____ a pool, in Aramaic called Bethesda, which _____ five roofed colonnades" (Jn.5:2).

3. "This he said to _____ by what kind of death he _____ to glorify God" (Jn.21:19).

4. The epistles of _____, _____, and _____ belong to the same time frame as the epistles of John.

5. False teachers are referred to as "men _____ in mind and _____ regarding the faith" (2 Tim.3:8).

6. False teachers with similar characteristics are cast into _____ _____ _____.

7. "You heard was coming and now _____ _____ _____ _____ already" (1 Jn.4:3).

8. "It _____ the _____ hour, and as you have heard that _____ is coming, so _____ many antichrists have come" (1 Jn.2:18).

9. "You have been _____ by the Holy One, and you all have _____" (1 Jn.2:20).

10. "You have no need that anyone should _____ you. But as his anointing teaches you _____ _____, and is true, and is no lie—just as it _____ taught you, abide in him" (1 Jn.2:27).

Match

1. The first martyred apostle
2. Pillar in the church
3. James
4. The right hands
5. Jews
6. Gentiles
7. Patmos
8. Hierapolis
9. Antichrists
10. Holy one

____ The Lord's brother
____ Circumcision
____ Residence of John
____ Church in Asia
____ John
____ Uncircumcision
____ False teachers
____ James
____ Unction
____ Of fellowship

LESSON 12

THE BOOK OF REVELATION

The Book of Revelation (65 or 66 A.D.)

The last book of our New Testament, and possibly the last book written, is the book of Revelation. When was it written, and how can we be certain of making the proper application of this book today? These are questions the understanding of which is essential to the comprehension of its message. In this brief space we cannot fully discuss these questions but will make only a brief attempt that will at least arouse our readers' interest.

The first suggestion that we shall make concerning this marvelous book is that it contains no new doctrines upon its pages. The Lord Jesus directed each of the seven churches of Asia to *"hear what the Spirit says to the churches"* (Rev.2:7,11,17,29; 3:6,13,22). What the Spirit said unto the churches *"it was declared at first by the Lord, and it was attested to us by those who heard, while God also bore witness by signs and wonders and various miracles and by gifts of the Holy Spirit distributed according to his will"* (Heb.2:3,4; cf.Jn.16:13; Acts 20:27). The Word was first revealed by the Holy Spirit unto inspired men and completed by the Jerusalem Conference in 49 or 50 A.D. After that time, the Holy Spirit continued to speak through inspired men while directing the writing of the New Testament Scriptures. We suggest that the book of Revelation was the last book of the New Testament revealed. It was revealed by an Angel and designed to give credibility to the other twenty-six books of the New Testament previously penned. The fulfillment of the events foretold by the Apocalypse established its own authenticity and that of all the other books of the Bible (cf.Rev.5:1-7).

Second, we emphasize that the book of Revelation was revealed to John by an Angel (Rev.1:1). The churches were already warned against receiving any thing revealed by an angel that constituted the revelation of new teaching (Gal.1:8,9). Nothing, therefore, in the book of Revelation could be received or accepted as from God that contained any revelation of new truth. All truth had been revealed no later than 50 A.D., or shortly thereafter. Therefore, the need for a late date for its writing is unwarranted. If the book contained nothing the early saints did not already know, why wait another thirty years to write it down?

Third, the book portrays prophetically historical occurrences which are (1) presented as fulfillment of the Old Testament prophets (Rev.10:7) and (2) the avenging of those prophets with the apostles (Rev.11:18; 16:6; 17:6; 18:20,24; 19:2). Daniel taught, *"Seventy weeks are decreed about your people and your holy city, to finish the transgression, to put an end to sin, and to atone for iniquity, to bring in everlasting righteousness, to seal both vision and prophet, and to anoint a most holy place"* (Dan.9:24). The Messiah would be cut off and the sacrifice caused to cease in the midst of the seventieth week. All of this would take place before the city and sanctuary were destroyed (Dan.9:25-27). Jesus refers to Daniel's prophecy in His Olivet discourse while describing the destruction of Jerusalem (Matt.24:15). He further said, *"For these are days of vengeance, to fulfill all that is written"* (Lk.21:22). The only things written when Jesus spoke were the Law and the Prophets. The Law and the Prophets contained the *"mystery of God would be fulfilled, just as he announced to his servants the prophets"* (Rev.10:7). Since the Apocalypse was designed to show *"things that must soon take place"* (Rev.1:1,19; 4:1; 22:6) in fulfillment of the mystery of God, it must, of necessity, predate 70 A.D.! To teach the Apocalypse was penned after 70 A.D. forces a contradiction between the two messages of Jesus. Furthermore, since the book portrays the avenging of the apostles and prophets (Rev.18:20), it must predate 70 A.D. because Jesus said the apostles and prophets would be avenged in the destruction of Jerusalem (Lk.11:45-52; Matt.23:34-39). If the apostles and prophets were avenged at Jerusalem, as Jesus said, how could they also be avenged elsewhere? To date the book of Revelation after 70 A.D. demands a double avenging of the apostles and prophets! A study of the nature of the avenging pictured by Jesus and John shows they are the same. These and many other convincing arguments demonstrate the Apocalypse was written prior to 70 A.D.

Fourth, the vision of chapters 4-11 explains the sealed scroll. The book was complete, written on both sides and sealed with seven seals (Rev.5:1). The Son of God took it from God's right hand (Rev.5:7) as He sent the Holy Spirit into all the earth (Rev.5:6). The emphasis here is upon the book and the seals. The seals reflected the authority of the book and its contents. Chapters 6-11 unveil the seals which depict historical events that give divine sanction to, and establish the authority of, the book. What are they? *"Things that must soon take place"* (Rev.1:1). Since these things symbolize the fulfillment of the Old Testament prophets (Rev.10:7) and avenging of the prophets and saints (Rev.11:18), the seals of necessity center around the historical developments that resulted in Jerusalem's destruction. A careful reading of the histories of Josephus will graphically portray the unfolding of these historical seals.

The book of Revelation and its prophecies do not end in the destruction of Jerusalem, however. Chapters 12-22 go beyond 70 A.D. picturing future events all the way to the judgment. However, for this book to serve its purpose of showing heaven's approval of God's revealed Word, contained also in written form, we must date it prior to 70 A.D.

The question of precisely when the book was written is much more difficult to answer. We know John wrote it while on the isle of Patmos *"on account of the word of God and the testimony of Jesus"* (Rev.1:9). We also know that in 65 A.D. Paul was a prisoner for the same reason (2 Tim.1:10-12). From all indications, John was on Patmos as a prisoner. The Lord's promise that he would prophesy again (Rev.10:11) indicates inactivity on John's part and gives credence to his being on Patmos as a prisoner. What conditions prevailed at this early date that would have demanded his imprisonment? The answer: the same conditions that demanded Paul's imprisonment. For some reason Paul, who appears to have been in Asia in 65 A.D., was arrested and sent to Rome for trial. The circumstances that demanded Paul's arrest would have likewise demanded John's. If John was taken to Ephesus, the provincial capital, for trial, as it appears Paul was, it would tell us why John was sent to Patmos. The authorities of Asia used this island prison to punish convicted criminals. John did not enjoy the privileges of Roman citizenship as did Paul (Acts 25:11). If John and Paul were victims of the same trials, one was sent to Rome and the other to Patmos. Apparently, most of the apostles were taken out of circulation about this time.

When the book of Revelation was written, tribulation among the saints of Asia had begun (Rev.1:9; 2:9) but had not reached the degree of suffering predicted by the Lord, Peter and others (Rev.3:9; cf.Dan.12:1; Matt.24:21; 1 Pet.4:12). The severity of the tribulation began to reach into these regions in 66 and 67 A.D.[41] This being the case, we would place the writing of the book of Revelation late in 65 or early 66 A.D. This means its writing was *before* the disturbances in Judea erupted into full-fledged war in the fall of 66 A.D. At that time, Cestus Gallus marched on Jerusalem, surrounded it and then fled back to Syria.[42] It also means the entire New Testament was written and in the hands of the Christians by this time. This chronology provides ample time for the Apocalypse to be written, copied and delivered to the churches of Asia and the rest of the world prior to fulfillment of the things foretold. There are many questions raised by these conclusions which cannot be answered in this short work.

Conclusion

We have followed the development of the New Covenant from its inception on Pentecost (Acts 2) as directed by its heavenly mediator, Christ, and executed by His chosen apostles of earth. The apostles, and other spiritually gifted persons, not only revealed Christ's will to their contemporaries by word of mouth but, by guidance of the same Spirit, recorded the New Covenant in written form. This writing constitutes the books known as the New Testament. None of these writings were available to those early believers for twenty or more years following Pentecost of 30 A.D. All of them, however, were completed *before* the destruction of Jerusalem. It is our studied conclusion that *"all things that pertain unto life and godliness"* and the *"exceeding great and precious promises"* were revealed *before* the destruction of Jerusalem in 70 A.D. (1 Cor.2:10-13; Eph.3:1-8). We further conclude that the book of Revelation was also written *before* these events occurred and deals with them as yet future when the apostle John wrote the Apocalypse. The New Testament in writing allows for the oral revelations prior to its completion while recording everything God chose to make permanent for succeeding generations till the end of time.

From the beginning, the Holy Spirit directed the apostles into *"all truth"* (Jn.16:13). He also directed others through the various spiritual gifts imparted by the laying on of the hands of apostles (1 Cor.12:1-11; Acts 8:17-19). He then inspired the writing of the New Testament Scriptures (2 Pet.3:15,16; 2 Tim.3:16,17). This inspiration was to continue until the whole package of truth was in written form, and then the inspiration of men by the Holy Spirit was to cease. Only three books of the New Testament existed when Paul said, *"Love never ends. As for prophecies, they will pass away; as for tongues, they will cease; as for knowledge, it will pass away. For we know in part and we prophesy in part, but when the perfect comes, the partial will pass away"* (1 Cor.13:8-10). Paul said the spiritual gifts would cease when *"when the perfect* (complete, AMO) *comes."* With the completion of the New Testament in written form, the inspiration of men ceased.

Long before Paul wrote, God spoke through Zechariah foretelling this very thing. He said, *"On that day there shall be a fountain opened for the house of David and the inhabitants of Jerusalem, to cleanse them from sin and uncleanness. And on that day, declares the LORD of hosts, I will cut off the names of the idols from the land, so that they shall be remembered no more"* (Zech.13:1,2). Note carefully that the fulfillment of this prophecy took place with the beginning of Christianity and that it foretold that the prophets would cease out of the land. Any prophecies thereafter would be lies (Zech.13:3,4). Since the context discusses the destruction of Jerusalem which took place in 70 A.D., the passing of the prophets would happen by that time. The message is the same as Paul's in 1 Corinthians 13:8. This being the case, the writing of the New Testament scriptures under the power of inspiration had to be completed prior to 70 A.D.

Lesson Exercises

True or False

1. ____ At one time, God's truth existed in both inspired men and the written word.

2. ____ The book of Revelation was revealed to John by the Holy Spirit.

3. ____ The book of Revelation gives credibility to all other N.T. books.

4. ____ Angels could reveal new truth even after the Jerusalem conference.

5. ____ A late dating for Revelation is needed to compensate for its revelation of new truth.

6. ____ Among other things, prophecy is history revealed before it happened.

7. ____ The book of Revelation was probably the last book of the Bible to be written.

8. ____ The Apocalypse foretold some events thousands of years yet future.

9. ____ Early believers had to wait only ten years after Pentecost to read the N.T.

10. ____ Every person in the world today has a Bible.

Lesson 12 - The Book of Revelation

Questions

1. At what point in time was the truth completely revealed?

2. What written things was Jesus talking about in Luke 21:22?

3. List a passage teaching that God would avenge the blood of the prophets in the destruction of Jerusalem:

4. What Jewish historian can assist us in our study of Revelation?

5. Were there any apostles arrested during the years of 65–66 A.D.?   Name one:

6. What privilege did Paul have that was not afforded John?

7. Explain why John would have been sent to Patmos while Paul was sent to Rome?

8. What passage teaches that spiritual gifts would cease?

9. What do you think **"the perfect"** refers to?

10. When did Zechariah say the prophet would cease out of the land?

Match

1. The Prophets
2. The Law
3. Apostles and Prophets
4. Sealed
5. Apocalypse
6. Holy Spirit
7. Christ
8. Laying on of hands
9. Exceeding great and
10. Life and

_____ Scroll
_____ Avenged
_____ Mediator
_____ Revealed Christ's will
_____ And the Prophets
_____ Godliness
_____ Precious promises
_____ Spiritual gifts
_____ God's Servants
_____ Book of Revelation

Multiple Choice

1. The churches of Asia were told to "hear what the **(Apostles, Jesus, Spirit)** saith."

2. At the first, the gospel began to be spoken by the **(Lord, Apostles, Spirit)**.

3. God bore witness to the gospel with **(signs and wonders, various miracles, gifts of the Holy Spirit)**.

4. John was on **(Patmos, Crete, Cyprus)** when he received the Apocalypse.

5. From all indications, John was on Patmos as a **(tourist, evangelist, prisoner)**.

6. Jerusalem was surrounded in 66 A.D. by Roman armies led by **(Cestus Gallus, Vespasian, Titus)**.

7. **(Three, Five, Twenty-five)** N.T. books were written before 1 Corinthians.

8. The invention of **(radio, television, printing)** made the scriptures more available.

Notes

LESSON 13

THE TESTIMONY OF HISTORY

In the previous lessons, we examined the revelation, development, production, reproduction, authority and completeness of our New Testament scriptures. Our study was based upon the internal evidence of the New Testament books themselves. We learned that God's truth was revealed to inspired men by the Holy Spirit. For the first twenty years, His truth resided in inspired men. Following the Jerusalem Conference, God's will began to be conveyed through the inspired page. The apostles took measures to ensure that the written word was accepted as equally authoritative as the spoken word (Acts 15:22-32; 2 Thess.2:15).

Our studies also unveiled design behind the written word and a plan for its reproduction and use. Christians were charged to make the written word available for all Christians to read (1 Thess.5:27) and they were charged to read each other's letters (Col.4:16). Christians followed these orders as evident from Peter's acknowledgment that he had read Paul's epistles (2 Pet.3:15,16). Paul and Peter taught that the word of God in inspired men would cease but would continue in the *writings* of inspired men (1 Cor.13:8-13; 2 Pet.1:12-15). These things show design and purpose behind the development of our New Testament scriptures. We believe our New Testament scriptures were given by the inspiration of God and furnish us completely unto every good work (2 Tim.3:16,17). They exist, not as an accident but as the result of God's divine purpose and grace.

Most Popular View

Our conclusion is not generally accepted in the religious world. Our New Testament scriptures are viewed more as the product of blind chance than the product of divine guidance. The following quotation will substantiate this fact:

> (1) The early Christians had in their hands what was a Bible to them, viz. the OT Scriptures. These were used to a surprising extent in Christian instruction. For a whole cent. after the death of Jesus this was the case. These Scriptures were read in the churches, *and there could be at first no idea of placing beside them new books which could for a moment rank with them in honor and authority.* It has been once and again discussed whether

> Christianity from the first was a 'book-religion.' The decision of the matter depends upon what is referred to by the word 'book.' Christianity certainly did have from the very beginning a book which it reverenced—the O.T.—but years passed before it had even the beginnings of a book of its own. What has been called 'the wealth of living canonical material,' namely prophets and teachers, made written words of subordinate value. In this very teaching, however, with its oral traditions lay the beginnings of that movement which was ultimately to issue in a cannon of writings. (2) When the actual work of writing began *no one who sent forth an epistle or framed a gospel had before him the definite purpose of contributing toward the formation of what we call 'the Bible.'... They had no thought of creating a new sacred lit. And yet these incidental occasional writings have come to be our choicest Scripture.*"[43]

Obviously, the thinking of denominational theologians differs from that reflected in this workbook. According to them, the New Testament Scriptures are the result of human ingenuity and not the product of divine purpose. This is reflected in other statements. For example, *"The history of the canon is the history of the process by which these books were brought together and their value as sacred Scriptures officially recognized. That process was gradual, furthered by definite needs, and, though unquestionably continuous, is in its earlier stages difficult to trace."*[44] The author of these statements contends that the books comprising our New Testament Scriptures were in existence in the first century but questions their existence as a unit. The effort of the historian has been to trace the development of the New Testament canon through different stages until it was evident that all twenty-seven books were together.

Canonization Theory

J. S. Riggs is the author of the I.S.B.E. article from which we quoted. He traces the evidence through three periods, (1) from the time of the apostles until 170 A.D., (2) from 170 to 220 A.D., and (3) the 3rd and 4th centuries A.D. The first two periods he views as the period of growth and development of the canon and the third period as the acceptance of the complete canon. This is probably the theory used by most Catholic and Protestant scholars in dealing with the canonization process of the New Testament Scriptures.[45]

Considering the Evidence

Riggs writes, *"By the end of the first century all the books of the N.T. were in existence."* The issue is not whether the books existed but whether they were collected as a unit (canon). He later wrote that *"a collection of the Pauline epistles existed at the time Polycarp wrote to the Phil and when Ignatius wrote his seven letters to the churches of Asia Minor, i.e. about 115 AD."* He also indicates there is evidence of the four Gospels being brought together in some places by this time.

Riggs looks at the writings of several noted persons in which they were influenced by numerous books of the New Testament. Clement of Rome (95 A.D., no one really knows when he lived) used material from Matthew and Luke. He was also influenced by the Epistle to the Hebrews and knew Romans, the Corinthian epistles, 1 Timothy, Titus, 1 Peter and Ephesians.

The epistles of Ignatius (115 A.D.) included corresponding references from the Gospels and language from Paul's epistles. His epistle to Polycarp made use of Philippians and nine other epistles of Paul. He also quoted from Matthew, 1 Peter and 1 John. This showed his acquaintance with these books.

Such works as *"The Teaching of the Twelve Apostles"* (120 A.D.), the *"Epistle of Barnabas"* (130 A.D.), and the *"Shepherd of Hermas"* (130 A.D.), exhibit the same things. They make references to the New Testament writings and quote from some of them. Again, this is evidence of the existence of the New Testament books.

In the years following, the *Apologists* came along defending Christianity against the state. Justin Martyr (100–165 A.D.) was the most prominent of the Apologists. He spoke of the Gospels as we speak of them today. One of his pupils, Tatian, made a harmony of our four Gospels. Martyr mentions the Apocalypse and appears to have known Acts, six epistles of Paul, Hebrews, 1 John and others.

In addition, certain heretics often use New Testament books to support their false teaching. Basilides, branded for heresy, used Matthew, Luke, John, Romans, 1 Corinthians, Ephesians and Colossians in support of his teaching. This man taught in Alexandria during the reign of Hadrian (117–138 A.D.). Valentinus made the same general use of the New Testament. Tertullian, a historian of the third century, informs us that Valentinus used the whole New Testament as it was then known.

Marcion, a noted Gnostic, went to Rome around 140 A.D. and became a heretic. In support of his error, he formed his own New Testament canon consisting of Luke and ten of Paul's epistles. He rejected the Pastoral Epistles, Hebrews, Matthew, Mark, John, Acts, the Catholic epistles and the Apocalypse. His acceptance and rejection of these books are clear evidence of the canonization of the New Testament Scriptures.

Other evidences cited by Riggs give a clear picture of the existence and use of our New Testament books following this period. Such names as Irenaeus (130-200 A.D.), Origen (185-254 A.D.), Cyprian (200-258 A.D.), and Eusebius (260-340 A.D.) all contribute evidence of the existence of our twenty-seven New Testament books. In 397 A.D., The Council of Carthage listed these books and decreed *"that aside from the canonical Scriptures nothing is to be read in church under the name of Divine Scripture."*

Which Came First?

As we observed, our N.T. Scriptures were together, as a whole, by the end of the 4th century. The evidence proves this, but the question must be raised, *"Does the evidence show the canon in the process of development, or does it show the existence of the canon?"* In other words, which came first, the canon or the evidence?

Riggs argued that the evidence showed the canon in development but acknowledged that it is impossible to say when and to what extent collections of our N.T. books began to be made. He admits that they were all written before the end of the 1st century. If the canon existed before the writers witnessed, the evidence proves the existence of the canon.

Evidence proves existence, not non-existence. To illustrate, I have in my possession a book by thirty different writers. If someone finds this book fifty years from now and quotes from ten of the authors, will that mean the other chapters in this book were not known to exist at the time. Absolutely Not!

In this workbook, we have quoted and cited many passages from Old and New Testament books proving we have access to these books. This does not prove, however, that we did not have the unused books of the Bible in our possession.

What Are the Facts?

We have already proved that the N.T. books themselves take note of the revelation process in the development of the New Testament Scriptures. Peter indicated he had read all of Paul's epistles written to that point in time (2 Pet.3:16). Paul quoted from Matthew and/or Luke indicating his knowledge of the existence of these books (1 Tim.5:18; cf.Matt.10:10; Lk.10:7). Luke said *"many have undertaken to compile a narrative of the things that have been accomplished among us"* (Lk.1:1) indicating he had access to those writings. Paul taught that spiritual gifts would cease *"when the perfect comes"* (1 Cor.13:10). Prophecy was to cease by the destruction of Jerusalem (Zech.13). Therefore, the complete package of truth in written form existed by 70 A.D., when Jerusalem was destroyed. No one can prove the existence of spiritual gifts after 70 A.D.

Conclusion

Our New Testament Scriptures are a divine production. They exist by the action of God. They are not here simply because early Christians desired to preserve their faith. They are here because God ordered and directed the development of the New Testament Scriptures. The evidence discussed showing their use in subsequent years is proof of their existence and substantiates the argumentation used in this presentation. The fact that a human council in 397 A.D. decreed them to be Scripture does not take away from what they already were. It rather upholds and sustains them for what they really are, the Word of God.

Today, a copy of the New Testament may be purchased in almost any store. It is the product of the mind of God, revealed to mankind by the Holy Spirit, and produced by the hands of divinely inspired men. It was reproduced by the combined efforts of uninspired men and preserved for us by the providence of God and the love of men who reverenced its pages. Every living mortal should read it, study it, respect it, believe it, and obey it. It is the WORD OF GOD.[46]

Lesson Exercises

True or False

1. _____ The first Christians only had the O.T. as a source of truth.
2. _____ Christians had both inspired men and writings between 50–70 A.D.
3. _____ The inspired man was the most authoritative.
4. _____ N.T. writers had no intention of creating a new sacred literature.
5. _____ Bible books must be officially recognized before joining the canon.
6. _____ By the end of the 1st century all N.T. books were in existence.
7. _____ Clement of Rome lived around 95 A.D. because he was one of the first Popes.
8. _____ Heretics often quoted from our N.T. books.
9. _____ The evidence proves that our N.T. canon was 250 years in the making.
10. _____ The Council of Carthage was convened by God.

Questions

1. In what way was the truth revealed between 30–50 A.D.?

2. In what way was the truth revealed between 50–70 A.D.?

3. In what way has the truth been made available since 70 A.D.?

4. When were spiritual gifts to cease?

5. What two things were Christians asked to do with the epistles written to them?

6. What does the word **canon** mean?

7. What council decreed our 27 N.T. books scripture, & when was this council held?

8. What approach do scholars generally take to canonization?

9. What evidence is there for early canonization?

10. In your opinion, was canonization early or late?

Lesson 13 - The Testimony of History

Fill In The Blank

1. _____ evidently read _____ epistles.

2. Polycarp had copies of the _____ epistles.

3. Ignatius included references from the _____ and language from _____ epistles in his writings.

4. Apologists defended Christianity against the _____.

5. _____ was a pupil of Justin Martyr.

6. Marcion was noted for the _____ heresy.

7. _____ quoted Matthew and/or Luke in 1 Timothy 5:18.

8. Luke said that _____ had set forth in order a declaration of those things believed among us.

9. Prophecy was to cease by the _____ ___ _____.

10. No one can prove the existence of _____ gifts after 70 A.D.

Match

1. Apologist
2. Tertullian
3. Jerusalem Conference
4. Marcion
5. Pastoral epistle
6. Council of Carthage
7. Catholic epistle
8. Hadrian
9. One of the Gospels
10. Ignatius

_____ 397 A.D.
_____ Titus
_____ Historian
_____ Jude
_____ Roman Emperor
_____ Justin Martyr
_____ John
_____ 115 A.D.
_____ Gnostic
_____ 49 or 50 A.D.

NOTES

1. Some of the conclusions reached in this study may be at variance with those reached by you as a student of the Word of God. Be assured the author does not seek to be different. I present the material contained herein with the fullest confidence that the conclusions reached are valid. I do not claim infallibility, however, and to err is human, even though I firmly believe in the accuracy, within proper latitude, of the conclusions reached. I ask only that each argument made and conclusion drawn be considered upon the strength of its scriptural soundness. If in error, I shall stand corrected. (AMO)

2. Thirty-one of the Old Testament books are quoted in the New Testament.

3. The International Standard Bible Encyclopedia, Septuagint, ed. James Orr, Vol. IV, (Grand Rapids, MI: Wm. B. Eerdmans Publishing Co, 1939), page 2722.

4. Joy, James Richard, Rome and the Making of Modern Europe (New York: Flood and Vincent, 1893), page 142.

5. Joy, Rome and Modern Europe, page 154.

6. Josephus, Flavious, Wars of the Jews, 2:7:3.

7. Zeitlin, Solomon, Who Crucified Jesus? (New York: Block Publishing Company, 1969), page 52.

8. Zeitlin, Who Crucified Jesus?, page 53.

9. Zeitlin, Who Crucified Jesus?, page 55.

10. Josephus, Flavious, Antiquities of the Jews, 19:8:2.

11. Zeitlin, Who Crucified Jesus?, pages 56-58.

12. Merivale, Charles, History of the Romans (New York: D. Appeton and Company, 1865), Vol. VI, page 423; Josephus, Antiquities, 20:7:1.

13. I.S.B.E., Procurator, Vol. IV, page 2458.

14. Josephus, Antiquities, 18:2:2; 18:4:2.

15. Rusk, Roger, The Day He Died (Christianity Today, March 29, 1974), pages 721-722.

16. 33 A.D. is the most commonly advocated date among churches of Christ for the year of our Lord's death and the subsequent beginning of Christianity. This date is reckoned by accepting A.D. 1 (the chronological dating system developed by Dionysius Exiguus in the early part of the 6th century A.D.) as the beginning point of the Christian era. It is dated from the birth of Christ. By adding the age of Jesus — He was 30 years of age at the beginning of His ministry (Lk.3:23) — to the 3½ years of His ministry, the year 33 A.D. is established. But Dionysius made a senseless mistake by dating the birth of Jesus four years after the death of Herod the Great, during whose reign Jesus was born (Matt.2:1-19; Lk.1:5). This means that the birth of Jesus took place at least four years prior to A.D. 1, leaving 30 A.D. in perfect harmony with the age of Jesus. The mistake of Dionysius, however, does not affect his computations of Roman history. It is only the inspired sacred record that must be rectified. (See Encyclopedia Britannica, Vol. 5, Chronology, page 728; The New Catholic Encyclopedia, Vol. IV, Dionysius Exiguus, page 877; I.S.B.E., Vol. I, Chronology of the New Testament, pages 644B-647).

17. Josephus, Antiquities, 20:7:1.

18. Merivale, History of Romans, Vol. VI, page 423, cf. footnote.

19. Josephus, Antiquities, 18:8:2-9.

20. Josephus, Antiquities, 19:5:1; 19:8:2.

21. Vine, W.E., An Expository Dictionary of New Testament Words, (Fleming H. Revell Company, 17th Impression, 1966), Vol. III, page 40.

22. Here and in later references all truth (also teaching, doctrine, revelation, law, etc.) is used to identify the New Testament law with all of its attending commandments, statutes and ordinances. This is not to say that the application of these principles was made to every situation that would develop. They had not. Even today we must apply these same principles (commandments) to differing situations. The law of Christ by which we determine right and wrong, however, was fully revealed before it was written in our New Testament Scriptures.

23. Vine, Expository Dictionary, Vol. III, page 174.

24. I.S.B.E., Galatia, Vol. II, page 1154.

25. Halley, Henry H., Bible Handbook, page 364.

26. Josephus, Antiquities, 20:9:1.

27. Vine, Expository Dictionary, Vol. III, page 173.

28. I.S.B.E., Acts of the Apostles, Vol. I, page 41.

29. Marshall, Alfred, The Interlinear Greek-English New Testament, (Grand Rapids, MI, Zondervan Publishing House), cf.Lk.1:3-4.

30. I.S.B.E., Epistle to the Ephesians, Vol. II, page 956.

31. The expression "they of Italy" has been interpreted by some to identify the brethren who were with Paul "from" Italy (cf. RSV, NEB, NIV, margin ASV, etc.), thus suggesting the author was not in Italy at the time of writing. This conclusion is permissible but not a necessary one. The same language could also have been used if the epistle was written from Italy. In fact, as Milligan points out, the expression would have been the most appropriate language someone of Paul's affinity could have used (Milligan, Robert, Epistle to the Hebrews, (Nashville, TN, Gospel Advocate Co., 1953), pages 385-386).

32. Vine, Expository Dictionary, Vol. I, apoluo, page 319; Vol. II, pages 331, 334.

33. Josephus, Antiquities, 20:8:5; 20:11:1.

34. Josephus, Wars, Preface:2.

35. Josephus, Wars, 2:13:4.

36. Merivale, History of Romans, Vol. VI, pages 128, 135, cf. footnote.

37. Marshall, Interlinear, Titus 3:1.

38. From The Open Bible, Copyright 1975 by Thomas Nelson, Inc., Publishers. Used by permission.

39. Josephus, Antiquities, 15:2:2; 15:3:1.

40. Marshall, Interlinear, John 21:19; cf.13:32; 16:14 where the same word (doxasei) is correctly translated in the future tense in our versions.

41. Josephus, Wars, 2:18:1-10.

42. Josephus, Wars, 2:19:1-7.

43. I.S.B.E., Canon of the New Testament, Vol. I, page 563 (Emphasis mine, AMO).

44. I.S.B.E., Canon of the New Testament, Vol. I, page 563.

45. The material presented in the next few paragraphs is taken from the I.S.B.E. as listed in the note above. We recommend that you read this article if it is available for you.

46. Every conclusion reached in this study cannot be supported by concrete evidence. We consider them close enough, however, that the general picture of the New Testament's development is correctly seen. We believe the use of this material in future Bible studies will greatly aid your understanding and enhance your learning experience.

www.ingramcontent.com/pod-product-compliance
Lightning Source LLC
Chambersburg PA
CBHW070313110426
42738CB00052B/2504